A to Z of Dreaming

A to Z of Dreaming

A comprehensive guide to understanding your dreams

LISA TENZIN-DOLMA

igloobooks.com

Lisa Tenzin-Dolma is the author of five non-fiction books, a novel, and a screenplay, and she has had over 300 articles published on a variety of subjects. Her special interests lie in psychology and the exploration of the untapped areas of the mind. Lisa lives in Bath, England.

Published in 2012
by Igloo Books Ltd
Cottage Farm
Sywell
NN6 0BJ
www.igloobooks.com

Cover picture kindly supplied by Corbis

This book was created for Igloo Books by
Amazon Publishing Ltd
7 Old Lodge Place
Twickenham
Middlesex TW1 1RQ

Author Lisa Tenzin-Dolma
Editor Ella Fern
Designers Maggie Aldred, Vivienne Brar
Illustrator Tamasin Boyer

CTP001 0812
2 4 6 8 10 9 7 5 3
ISBN 978 0 85780 532 4

Printed and manufactured in China

Contents

The World of Dreams

The Nature of Dreams

Dreams are mysterious and often elusive. Some vanish even before we have fully woken, and others can haunt us for years. They can be bizarre, terrifying, joyful or confusing. We are able to have experiences in dreams that we could never expect to have in waking life. Our senses are heightened, and we are able to enter realms where the seemingly impossible is commonplace, and time has no meaning.

Dreams have the power to heal, foretell the future, inform us, or confound us. If we dive beneath the surface of this world of sleep that we all inhabit for a large section of our lives, we can access a treasure-trove of information that our waking mind is oblivious to.

Why we dream

Almost a third of our lives is taken up with sleeping, and one fifth of that sleep time is spent in the dream-state. Even though some people have no recollection of this in their waking hours, everybody experiences dreams. If you were deprived of sleep, and therefore of dreams, you would initially become disoriented and confused, and ultimately your mental and physical health would suffer, because dreaming is essential to your wellbeing. It sorts, sifts, clarifies and ultimately illuminates the large, small and even seemingly invisible happenings of everyday life.

While you are awake, you are constantly being bombarded with information in the form of experiences, thoughts, actions, reactions, and sensory impressions. All of this information needs to be sifted, processed, categorised and added to your vast store of conscious and subconscious memories. Some can be dealt with immediately, through decision-making, insights and practical application. More subtle information is relegated to the subconscious mind, where it remains. Some of this information lies silently, forever buried, but a great deal of it is sorted through and put to use while you sleep. The subconscious mind is the vehicle that takes you to increased self-knowledge, if you know how to access its secrets.

The subconscious mind is a storehouse of information, too chaotic to be clearly understood by the conscious mind. If you imagine your mind as a vast ocean, the conscious mind would be the surface of the water. Any activity here is clearly visible. Thoughts come and go like boats in a regatta, negotiating around each other, drawing together to make connections and facilitate exchanges. Beneath the surface of the ocean it may appear to be quiet and still; the water there is apparently undisturbed by the activity that takes place above. Yet flotsam, jetsam and treasure are hidden here. Predators and strange unknown creatures lurk, ready to terrify us when we disturb them. Creatures of great beauty and luminosity shimmer secretly, waiting for our call. All of these eventually rise to the surface and interconnect with the traffic that passes by. The subconscious mind deals with this; with the thoughts and impressions that we push aside, and with the feelings that, for various reasons, are not openly acknowledged, and are instead buried deep. The currency of the subconscious mind, and its 'group aspect', the collective unconscious, is very different to that of the rational processes of the conscious mind, which is used for thoughts or words that are immediately recognisable. The subconscious mind deals in the arcane areas of symbolism and imagery, and it has the power to alchemically transform hidden memories, barely-noticed feelings or impressions, into dreamscapes that fix our attention and insist that we take notice.

Your dreams are messengers from the subconscious. They help you to recognise and interpret the information and subtle impressions that filter through to the subconscious mind. Your hidden feelings about yourself and others, your inner conflicts, fears, worries, hopes and desires are all filed away beneath the surface. They may be forgotten by the conscious mind, but the subconscious has a long and tenacious memory. Dreams are powerful things; they can be shocking and frightening, healing and cleansing, illuminating and even prophetic, and can alert you to previously unrecognised aspects of yourself. By taking notice of your dreams, you can understand yourself and your environment more effectively.

Types of dreams

Your dreams perform specific functions that can be divided into categories, and these are connected with how you are feeling mentally, emotionally and

physically. Overlaying these various expressions of your subconscious mind are what Carl Jung termed 'big' and 'little' dreams. The 'big' dreams are those that are immediately recognised as important and significant. These bring about insights, and an understanding of major changes that are being experienced in your life. The 'little' dreams are nudges from your subconscious mind that prompt you to acknowledge and deal with emotions or minor situations that are currently being ignored. Both 'big' and 'little' dreams can be focused through the lens of the same dream categories. These categories are: processing, dealing with emotions, spiritual insights, prophetic dreams, and lucid dreaming.

Processing dreams enable you to confront your feelings over changes that you are experiencing, or issues that you are facing. One of the most common themes in processing dreams is anxiety, manifested by worries for which your conscious mind is not currently able to find a solution. Concerns over relationships, health, work, finances, exams, are all brought to the surface through processing dreams. These dreams may be repeated over and over, sometimes with variations in slightly differing forms, called recurring dreams, until you are able to consciously take steps to deal with the problem. Times of great change can bring about processing dreams which prompt you to face your anxieties. If you look at them with an eye fixed on the signs and symbols that they offer you, they can provide clues which will enable you to find solutions.

Emotions that are not readily acknowledged or accepted, and instead are denied or repressed, give rise to emotional dreams. These magnify your inner feelings in ways that can be intense and uncomfortable. Fears are confronted through nightmares, and common motifs are terrifying dreams of being attacked or pursued, or trapped with no apparent escape route. Anxiety can spark dreams in which you are panicking about being late for a meeting, or are among a crowd of people, and realise with horror that you are naked. In times of stress, your dreams can provide an outlet for buried feelings, and can act as a safety-valve. Feelings of frustration, anger, fear or envy that you would prefer not to face are brought to your attention while you sleep. Powerful emotions can bring about pleasant dreams as well, such as dreaming of a lover, or being in a beautiful place.

Closely affiliated with dreams about your own hidden feelings are dreams of other people reacting towards you in a manner that seems unlikely in waking life. Your subconscious, like an antenna, picks up signals

★★

from messages such as body language or tones of voice. Dreaming that a friend is acting in a hostile manner towards you could mean that either your insecurities around the relationship are being revealed, or that you are subliminally picking up messages about hidden undercurrents within the relationship. You can use these warning signals to face the situation, and clarify what is truly happening.

Illumination in the form of spiritual insights can come through dreams. Just as your subconscious mind is a repository for information, it can also be a point of connection with the Superconscious, your Spiritual Self. Insights come in flashes, brief ignitions that traverse the link between the mundane and the spiritual, and these can change your entire view of the world and your place in it. Included within the realm of spiritual dreams are creative dreams that open the gateway to new spiritual, artistic and scientific knowledge. Albert Einstein's dream of riding on a beam of light gave rise to the Theory Of Relativity. The German chemist, Friedrich von Kekule, discovered the structure of the Benzene molecule through a dream in which a snake was swallowing its tail. The paintings of some artists are often inspired by their dreams. You may hear beautiful music that sends your soul soaring even after you wake.

Prophetic dreams are not reserved only for the domain of mystics. Time as we measure it does not exist in the dream-state, and dreams can provide glimpses into the future, especially in situations where heightened emotions are present. Prophetic dreams can range from meetings with future partners to large-scale disasters that send ripples through the consciousness of whole populations.

Lucid dreams contain images that appear to be more luminous and 'real' than ordinary dreams. Within these, there is a sense of intense alertness alongside an awareness that you are dreaming, and this allows you to control what happens within the dream. If you pay attention to your dreams and keep a journal, you will find that lucid dreams become more common, to the extent that you can choose what you will dream about in order to either problem-solve or to follow particular pathways within your mind. Lucid dreams can even help you to feel more self-empowered in your waking life, because the thought becomes seeded that if you can control a dream, that most nebulous state, then you can take control in areas of your waking life that you may not have previously considered.

Levels of sleep

There are four different phases of sleep, and each one is reflected through changes in the rhythms of your brain waves. These rhythms govern different aspects of your waking and sleeping life, and are measured in hertz, or cycles per second. The higher beta state of sixteen to thirty-two cycles per second comes into use in situations of intense emotions such as excitement or fear. The lower beta state resonates at a frequency of twelve to sixteen cycles per second. This is associated with speaking, learning skills, and relating to others. The alpha state resonates at eight to twelve cycles per second, and is associated with a relaxed, thoughtful, passive state of mind. The theta state of four to eight cycles per second is utilised during light sleep and deep meditation, where there is a sense of ease and tranquillity, and your mind drifts. The delta state consists of waves of one-half to four cycles per second, and is associated with deep sleep.

In the first stage of sleep, the beta waves, which indicate ordinary waking consciousness, change to alpha waves, and you experience a drifting sensation, lowered blood pressure and pulse, and muscle relaxation. Fleeting images, that are part of your processing of the previous day, occur as your mind slows down and prepares for sleep. The second stage is that of light sleep, which is characterised by theta waves, and this moves into the Rapid Eye Movement (REM) stage which signals the dream state. Twenty to forty minutes later, you slip into the delta phase which signifies deep sleep. These phases of sleep are repeated three or four times, and the REM phase, though initially very brief, lengthens as you move through the repeated sleep stages. Your final REM phase can last for up to an hour, and if you are woken during this stage you will have a clear recollection of your dreams. Although it sometimes feels as if you have been in a dream all night, generally only up to two hours of your total sleep period is spent dreaming.

Hypnagogic and Hypnopompic states

During the first phase of sleep, just as you are drifting off, you experience random images that flit through your mind's eye. These may be of faces or landscapes, spiritual images or even pieces of music, and are indicative of the Hypnagogic state. It is as though your mind is scanning your brain, sifting, recollecting, and looking for some kind of order, and usually the images or music that are played inwardly to you at this time are unfamiliar.

★★

You may even feel certain that you are not actually asleep, but instead are merely relaxing. At this time your mind is opening itself to the images that will come through in your dreams.

The Hypnopompic state is the transition between sleeping and waking, and it is while you are in this phase that dreams stay in your memory and can be recalled. It is the most creative phase of sleep, as you can use this state to make connections with the symbolism occuring in your dreams, and can be guided by this in your waking life. Because the Hypnopompic stage is passed through very quickly, lying quietly for a few minutes on waking and keeping a dream journal can help you to retain and make sense of the images from your dreams.

What you can learn from your dreams

Your dreams are a pathway to the Deep Self. They can reveal your hidden hopes, fears and motivations, and can help you to better understand yourself. Some of your dreams have messages that can be taken literally, such as dreams of illness that warn you to take extra care of your health, or serve to bring inner worries to the surface through magnifying them. Others are projections of inner feelings. Yet others have a symbolic or spiritual meaning that needs to be decoded in order to be understood. A dream dictionary can help you to decipher the messages from your dreams, but your personal interpretation of these is also very important.

The History of Dreams

The interpretation of dreams has a long history, and has been accorded tremendous significance. Ancient Egypt is thought to be the first place where dream incubation, the act of dreaming in order to deliberately access messages from the subconscious mind, was put into practice, and the first written record of dream interpretation dates back to 1350 BC in Egypt. In Greece, Hippocrates, the father of medicine who lived from 469–399 BC, wrote 'On Dreams', in which he expounded his theory that while awake, the soul receives images, and while asleep, the soul produces images that we recognize as dreams. The Greeks firmly believed that healing could come through dreams, and the temple at Delphi, with its instruction to 'Know Thyself' set above the entrance, was used partly for this purpose. In 4 AD, 'The Five Books Of Dream Interpretation' was written by the Greek sage Artemidorus, and many of his interpretations are still considered valid today.

The Assyrians believed that dreams were omens, and interpreted them as being predictions of future events. In China, the soul was considered to fly free during dreams, communicating with the spirits of the dead.

In Japan, the Emperor slept in a special dream chamber in order to more clearly receive messages from the spirit world. In Malta, underground chambers, dedicated to that purpose, were used for dream incubation. The Hypogeum, an underground sanctuary in Malta, encompasses 6,000 square metres on three levels. Beyond the main hall is an oracle room, a dreaming chamber where a priestess would lie down to sleep and incubate dreams. Statues of dreaming priestesses have been discovered in the chamber.

Priests and Priestesses within the Babylonian, Mesopotamian, Hittite, Hebrew, Druid, Native American, Aboriginal, Taoist, Buddhist, and early Christian traditions all interpreted dreams as part of their spiritual duties. Solomon, Jacob, Nebuchadnezzar and Joseph were all visited by a prophet or deity who gave instructions that influenced decision-making. The Talmud, written between 200 and 500 AD, includes over two hundred references to dreams. Since the dawn of humankind, dreams have been viewed as tools for self-knowledge, and in many cultures there are still 'dream advisors' who are able to dispense advice and make predictions.

Although dreams were viewed in the past as messages from a higher power, they became an accepted aspect of psychology when Sigmund Freud and Carl Jung included the significance of dreams in their writings about psychological diagnoses and theories. Freud believed that dreams were disguised messages that revealed hidden desires, often dormant since childhood. Jung surmised that dreams are sometimes images from the collective unconscious, the pool of memories and experiences common to all humanity, and can teach us a great deal about ourselves. Jung taught that one of the ways in which dreams could be interpreted is through viewing each character and element as an aspect of the dreamer's personality. Understanding the symbols within dreams could lead to a more integrated personality. One aspect of this is a recognition that 'archetypes' – instinctual mental images or imprints that inhabit the collective unconscious and are common to all cultures – are present within dreams. Our relationship with these archetypes is played out through dreams. In this case, the wise old man or woman, the fearsome shadow aspect, or the lover, are all aspects of yourself that come to you in your dreams with a message for you.

The onset of technology, with EEG machines that can track and record the patterns made by brainwaves, has increased the scientific understanding of which phase of sleep is vital for dreaming. Whereas in the past dreams were considered to be a method of communing with higher forces or of acknowledging suppressed emotions, now it is recognised that dreams are vital to the maintenance of mental and physical health.

The language of dreams

The language of dreams is symbolic, because dreams reflect the subconscious, collective unconscious, and the Superconscious aspects of the Self, and these aspects communicate through images rather than words. Yet the language that your dreams speak is an intrinsic part of you, and with practice, you can learn to decode it easily. The most important element is that of recognising the symbols. Once you can recollect the symbols that appear in your dreams, and consider the feelings that these engendered in you, the first step to clear interpretation has been accomplished.

Dreams are often a series of jumbled images, so in order to separate these and interpret them, you can first of all consider the environment that you find yourself in during your dream. If, for instance, it is a school or college, you will know that you can relate the symbols in your dream to a learning environment in your present situation. Note whether you are in a situation in your waking life that you need to pay attention to, and learn from. Think about how you view these establishments in waking life. Your feelings and sensations within the dream are an indicator of how you inwardly feel about the waking environment. Are you nervous or afraid in your dream? If so, perhaps you have been repressing your fears or anxieties in daily life. Are you in receipt of a prize or accolade in your dream? If so, your hopes are being revealed, or a secret inner conviction is surfacing.

Your inner feelings set the tone for the symbols that occur in your dreams. If you are building a wall in a dream, you could explore whether you really wish to shut yourself off from something or someone in your waking life. If you are knocking down a wall, you are breaking down a barrier that separates you from new experience.

The colours you see in your dreams are significant. Are they vibrant, or dull? What do those colours represent to you? When people appear in your dreams, are they already known to you? How does their behaviour in waking life differ from how they appeared in the dream? How did you feel towards

★★

them in the dream, compared with your usual waking feelings about them?

Each dream is interpreted according to the dreamer. Driving a car in a dream takes on a different significance for a non-driver, who may be nervous about it, than for a driver who views this as commonplace, yet the dream for both people symbolises taking control of your life. The symbols found within dreams are universal, but your inner feelings about that symbol are what lend relevance to your interpretation. Many dreams, however, have a clear meaning when they are divided into sections and looked at carefully.

Guide to two levels of interpretation

In this book, two levels of interpretation are used that will help you to understand the messages that your dreams hold for you. If you look at a dream as though it is a story, this will help you to find a beginning, middle and end, and to seek out the sometimes complex sub-plot that can carry deep significance. Level **1** of interpretation describes the motifs of the dream and its basic meaning, and Level **2** helps you to look for deeper, more subtle symbolism that can shed light on the spiritual 'story' within your dream. The interpretations in the Dream Dictionary can help you to decipher your hidden feelings or reactions, hopes and concerns, through the symbols that are revealed during your dreams. Both levels of interpretation can be valuable in uncovering the meaning of your dream.

The Dream Diary pages at the end of this book can help you to understand the initial impressions that you receive from a dream, and this can pave the way for deeper insights, because the diary enables you to focus on the motifs as well as the feelings that these symbols engendered. If you only remember snatches of your dream on waking, writing in your dream diary will help you to recall your dream in more detail later on.

The initial questions to ask yourself are:

- What was the dream story?
- Were you a participant or an observer in the dream?
- What were your actions or reactions to the events?
- What were the main characters and images you remember?
- Were any of the dream characters familiar to you?
- Did anything in the dream strike you as particularly significant?
- Where or when was the dream set?
- How did it make you feel?
- Your interpretation

★★

Case study

I was in a classroom, all alone. I looked for my friends, and couldn't see anyone. I felt sad and lonely, and wasn't sure what to do or where to go. Then I saw a face I recognised at the window, and suddenly realised that there was a door in the wall that led outside. I went through the door, and into the playground, where I saw a group of my friends all in a huddle. I wasn't sure whether to go to them or not, but one of them called me over. When I joined them, someone started to be unkind to me, but another girl made it clear that I should stay, so I felt comfortable about staying there.

I woke up feeling happy.

Interpreting this dream using Level **1**, it is clear that there are at least four main motifs. The classroom indicates that this is a learning situation for the dreamer. The feeling of isolation illustrates a loneliness that is being reflected through the dream. The door is an opening into a new realm of experience, should the dreamer choose to take it. The group indicates acceptance, even if not everyone is friendly.

Combining this with Level **2** of dream interpretation, it is clear that, whether the dreamer is an adult or a child, the overriding atmosphere of this dream is a deep-seated need for acceptance by peers. The classroom is a learning situation, which signifies that the dream's purpose is to teach something to the dreamer. Initially the atmosphere of the dream is lonely – there is a sense of isolation – and this is later borne out by the initial reluctance to join the group of peers. A face appears at the window, the vision out into the world, and a doorway, a path forward, is then recognised. By passing through the doorway, the dreamer is choosing to take a step towards a larger world than the one that is currently being inhabited. Once the dreamer has joined the group, one person is unwelcoming, but another is friendly, and the dreamer chooses to acknowledge this, and stay. The decision brings a feeling of happiness that lasts after the dreamer has woken.

This dream was experienced by a girl on the edge of puberty, a time when acceptance by peers is an essential aspect of life. After we had discussed the dream and interpreted it together, she agreed with great excitement that she had been afraid of being 'left out', but had been nervous about taking steps that would lead to inclusion in a group of friends. She determined to be more outgoing, and this helped her to develop new friendships and increase her self-confidence. The interpretation would be just as relevant for an adult.

★★★

The archetypes in dreams

An archetype is an instinctual mental imprint that rests deep within the Collective Unconscious. Archetypes are common to all cultures, and their imprints were laid down early in humankind's evolution. Each of us recognises these archetypes, whether consciously or unconsciously. The Mother, the Child, the Wise Sage, the fearsome Shadow element are all primal aspects of ourselves. Some of these may be so deeply buried that they only surface in dreams, brought to waking consciousness through the mind's attempts to grapple with a problem, deal with intense emotions, or remind us of aspects of ourselves that are being ignored. Depending upon our cultural conditioning and philosophical beliefs, we give different names and personalities to these archetypes. For example, the Great Mother in her positive, nurturing aspect may be Mary or Isis; in her demonised, destructive aspect she may be Kali, or Lilith.

Within the realm of archetypes is the triumvirate of the Male, Female, and Essential Self that are all intrinsic aspects of each individual. Our perspective of relating comes through the Ego, our seat of observation and mode of connecting to reality that makes judgements and decisions. The elements that we deny surface as the Shadow. The Male and Female aspects reveal themselves as the Anima and Animus, and in dreams these always appear as a member of the opposite sex from the dreamer.

The Anima is the female aspect within a man, and reveals itself as a woman in male dreams. It governs the traditionally feminine qualities of gentleness, receptivity, intuition and compassion. The Anima encompasses a man's ideals around women, and the qualities that he finds most attractive and appealing. It is set in motion from the first moment of relationship with a mother-figure, and characterised by the qualities of every woman he meets throughout life. When the Anima is neglected or suppressed in waking life, a man may stifle feelings of tenderness, gentleness or compassion, and this will surface through dreams as a reminder to integrate both elements of the Self more fully.

The Animus is the male aspect within a woman. It governs the elements of logic, practicality, and objectivity. In dreams it appears as a masculine figure, and encompasses the ideals around every man a woman has encountered, from the father-figure onwards. If a woman has neglected or

★★

cut off her association with the Animus, this will be revealed in dreams as a reminder to reconnect with its presence. At times when a woman is unsure of herself, or doubts her powers of judgement or deduction, she may stifle her active energy and drive. At these times the Animus surfaces and makes its presence felt in dreams, as a reminder to identify more fully with both sides of the personality, and to integrate these within the psyche.

Case study

I dreamed that I was asleep on a sofa, after a party. In the dream, I woke and noticed that a beautiful young woman was lying on the floor, close to me. I sat up and leaned over her, and found, to my absolute horror, that she was dead. I panicked. For some reason I was certain that somehow I had killed her, although I had no memory of seeing her before. I woke from the dream feeling utterly distraught.

Using Level **1** of interpretation, the motifs are those of dreaming about being asleep, waking up, the beautiful woman, the apparent death, and the panic. Level **2** of interpretation reveals the true feelings of the dreamer, and the recognition of the Anima.

The young man who recounted this dream was searching for meaning because it had upset him terribly and he could not shake the memory of it. He was engaged in a long period of intense study that had required the full extent of his logical and deductive powers, and this had entailed setting aside his customary gentle, intuitive nature in order to focus completely on his logical self. When it was suggested to him that the female in the dream was his Anima reminding him that he was 'killing off' the sensitive, feminine aspects of himself by ignoring them, he agreed that he had been neglecting these, and determined to focus a little more on those suppressed elements.

You can learn a great deal about how you relate to the opposite sex, both internally and externally, through observing how the Anima and Animus behave in your dreams. Consider whether an element in your nature is being repressed or ignored to the extent that it has to 'stand out' to be noticed. You will find that, through exploring what might be currently missing in your life, the figures in your dreams will reflect your increasing self-understanding and the integration that can then naturally take place. Through your acknowledgement of all aspects of yourself, even dreams that were unpleasant in tone can now act purely as messengers from your Deep Self. By entering into what is termed the 'Sacred Marriage', the union of the male and female aspects of yourself, you can fully embrace both sides of your nature. The mystery lover who you feel so intrinsically connected with is actually part of you.

THE ESSENTIAL SELF is your true inner nature, the embodiment of your soul. It reminds you, through your dreams, of your innate potential, your creativity, and your ability to be the orchestrator of your life. The Essential Self is the 'real' you; the essence of your thoughts and actions. It has no agenda other than to remind you of the Spiritual Self who resides beneath the layers of personality in which you are clothed.

Often the Essential Self appears as a luminous dream figure at times of great stress, and takes the guise of guide or advisor. You may experience the Essential Self as a holy figure, a spiritual teacher with whom you identify, or even a god or goddess. It can manifest as a meaningful symbol, or a sense of total 'knowing', benevolence, and unconditional love. The connection with the Essential Self can be strengthened by systems such as meditation that enable you to perceive deeper layers of being.

THE SHADOW is the aspect of yourself that is buried, neglected, denied or thwarted. We each contain every trait known to humanity within the psyche. The elements that you reject in others as unsavoury, distasteful, or downright nasty become the Shadow. For a pacifist, the Shadow may be a murderer, or a militant. For a courageous person, the Shadow may be a coward. The Shadow is the sum of your dreads and fears; of the most destructive elements of the personality that are never allowed to surface in waking life. All of the qualities or characteristics that you abhor in others will be present as the Shadow within. In dreams, you may find that the Shadow also appears within the archetypal figures; for instance, the Shadow of the Nurturing mother is the Destructive mother.

By facing the Shadow through acknowledging its presence, this aspect of yourself loses its power, and gradually disappears from your dreams. It does not need expression, but it desires recognition and acceptance, without being played out in everyday life. The battle between the many aspects of the Self is then no longer an issue, and the nightmares that bring this to your attention are no longer needed as a pointer to inner conflicts that seek resolution.

★★★★★★★★★★★★★★★★★★★★★★★★★★★★★★★★★★★★★★★

Characters in dreams

There are two ways in which you can view the characters who appear in your dreams, and it is useful to employ both of these in your interpretation. Firstly, you can view each character as an aspect of yourself. Even animals, the landscape, the time of day, and the season can give you pointers into your inner feelings, hopes, fears, desires and motivations. The second method of interpretation is to examine any undercurrents that are flowing between yourself and other people in your life, as there may be unspoken tensions, or deep connections that you are reluctant to acknowledge or deal with.

Case study

I was in a field with my mother and a man I don't know in waking life, but to whom I felt very close in the dream. There were spring flowers around us, the light was beautiful, and I felt relaxed and happy. We all sat on the grass, and I started to unpack food and drink from a bag I was carrying. Then my mother began to argue about everything I laid out. Nothing was as she wanted it, and I was very upset because I'd made an effort to make this a good day. The man calmly tried to defuse the situation by saying what nice food I'd brought. When my mother refused to be mollified, he took my hand and pointed out a hare that was running very fast across the field, away from us.

Interpretation using Level **1** includes the motifs of the field, the mother, the familiar man, the flowers, the food and drink, the conflict, and the hare. Level **2** also brings in the beautiful light, which indicates that this is an important or 'big' dream, and the support of the man who is clearly the Animus.

When the dream is interpreted in the context of each element as an aspect of the Self, the dreamer is clearly allowing her Inner Critic, represented by her mother, to influence her and upset her. The dreamer wants to 'do the right thing' in her waking life, but is afraid that she will 'get it wrong' or is 'not good enough'. The mother who is scathing about the dreamer's efforts with the picnic is the Shadow aspect of the dreamer's nurturing Mother archetype, and manifests the Inner Critic whose destructive influence saps the dreamer's confidence. The man is the dreamer's Animus, who reminds her to be assertive without being aggressive, and who points out the hare, which represents both intuition, and the ability to move swiftly away from threatening situations. The season in the dream is springtime, indicating new beginnings that lead to growth. The food is emotional and mental, as well as physical, nourishment, and reminds the dreamer to nurture herself on all levels, regardless of outside opinions.

While exploring the meaning of the dream through relationships with people from waking life, the dreamer commented that although she wishes to be closer to her mother, she frequently feels criticised. The issue over food in the dream is, in essence, an inner conflict over the lack of a nurturing relationship with her mother, which she is trying to improve even though she is afraid of rejection. Because the loving man in her dream was a stranger, he is clearly her Animus, and is a reminder from her logical Self that the heightened emotions between herself and her mother can best be dealt with by stepping back. She can assess the relationship, retreat like the hare in the dream if necessary, and help matters further through adopting a calm attitude.

Recalling your dreams

The more you pay attention to your dreams, the easier it will be to remember them and learn from them. You may find that you can remember snatches of dreams, brief glimpses that leave you with a feeling rather than an understanding of what the dream was about. By training yourself to recall your dreams, you will find that even if you cannot remember a dream immediately upon waking, fragments of it will remain, and the full details of the dream will be sparked by something later on. The two easiest methods of ensuring that you will recall your dreams are to create the most conducive sleeping environment, and to keep a dream diary.

Your environment

Your bedroom should be a place of sanctuary that facilitates restful sleep and provides a helpful environment for dreaming and remembering your dreams. Avoid unnecessary clutter, and, if possible, use your bedroom only for sleeping. When your bedroom is utilised for working, or watching television, your mind is kept active. This can prevent you from settling down to peaceful sleep, and can interfere with the clarity of your dreams. If possible, have curtains that fully shut out the light while you are in bed, so that you sleep more deeply. Use an alarm clock that wakes you gently, as this will ensure that your dreams are not banished instantly.

★★★★★★★★★★★★★★★★★★★★★★★★★★★★★★★★★★★★★★★

Before you go to bed, take a few minutes to unwind. Play soothing music, or meditate, and review the day in your mind. If you are relaxed and clear-headed before sleep, your dreams can act as keys that help you to discover solutions, and can enable you to gain a deeper self-understanding.

You may find it helpful to scent your bedroom with essential oils or pot-pourri, or to hang a Native American dreamcatcher above your bed. A dreamcatcher is believed to capture unpleasant dreams in its web, while allowing the helpful dreams to slip through and be remembered.

Keeping a dream diary

A dream diary is an invaluable aid to remembering and interpreting your dreams. Keep a dedicated notebook and pen by your bed, so that you can write down your dreams as soon as you wake. Use the Dream Diary at the end of this book to start you off at recording your dreams. It will help you remember your dreams and begin interpreting them.

Before you go to sleep, write down the day and date for the following day in your diary. This will act as a trigger for dreams. You can train your subconscious mind to bring you dreams that you will remember in detail.

If you wake from a dream during the night, jot down the details of your dream in brief, and then add to this in the morning. If you find it difficult to go back to sleep after you have written down your dreams during the night, you could dictate them into a small tape recorder kept close by, and then transcribe your memories and impressions into your journal in the morning.

When you write down your memories of a dream, think about all aspects of it. Who were the characters in your dream? Are they known to you, or are they strangers, or animals, or other-worldly beings? Were you actively present in the dream, or an observer? Write down the events of the dream in sequence. What was happening? Where did it take place? What were you doing, and how did you feel? Was the light in your dream diffuse, or clear? Was there an impression of a particular time of day, or season?

Now examine what each of these elements mean to you personally. Divide the dream into sections, and look at these individually. Record your feelings about the various elements in each section of the dream. For instance, if you dreamed about a dog, how do you feel about dogs generally? A dream about a dog barking can be a warning about something or someone you need to be wary of in your current waking situation. Depending upon the atmosphere in the dream, a barking dog could be your protector or guardian, or it could represent a person or situation that you feel 'dogged' or 'hounded' by. A friendly dog can be an ally, a protector, a faithful companion in your life, or even a playmate. If you are usually nervous of dogs, it is important to consider how you felt about the dog in your dream. Ask yourself whether you felt comfortable with the dog, how you interacted with it, and what this tells you about yourself and people in your acquaintance that you feel the dream could be connected with.

Your dreams are rich in symbols, because the subconscious mind makes its presence felt through symbolism and imagery, so your personal interpretation is vital to your understanding of the messages of your dreams.

Finally, look at the overview, and analyse your dream according to current situations or events in your life. It may be that you are being shown a solution to a problem, or that your dream reveals your true feelings about your circumstances, and brings to the surface your anxieties, hopes or wishes.

If you do not remember any dreams in the morning, write down how you felt upon waking. This will help you to develop a habit of keeping your dream journal, and may even prompt you to remember them later on, as well as encouraging you to remember future dreams.

Case study

I dreamed that I was giving birth. A woman was present in the room, but she was blurry and indistinct, and hovered in the background. She took no part in the actual delivery process. It was very easy to bring this baby into the world – I experienced no pain, just a few cramps that were only slightly uncomfortable. I felt completely unruffled by the labour and birth – I just took it as a matter of course, and delivered the baby (a girl) myself.

This dream was very significant to the dreamer, who had just acted on a major decision to go self-employed as a freelance journalist. She had been very nervous about this, and had expressed worries about whether she would be able to earn a living working independently. Her dream reassured her that she had made the right decision. Interpreting this dream using Level **1**, the central motifs are birth, the midwife, the baby, and lack of pain. The Level **2** interpretation clarified that the 'new life' she was bringing into being was a fresh and joyful phase in her own life, rather than a literal child. She had always called work projects her 'babies', and the girl baby represented fresh creativity and productivity through her own efforts. The easy birth indicated that her career change would go smoothly. The woman

★★★

in the background did not act as midwife, and the dreamer felt that this was someone in her working life who could be helpful in promoting the work she was currently engaged in. In order to understand her dream, she divided it into sections in her dream journal. This is her entry.

Date: 11th February
What was the dream story?
It was about giving birth to a daughter, without help from a midwife.
Were you a participant or an observer in the dream?
An active participant.
What were your actions or reactions to the events?
I delivered the baby myself, and felt very strong and capable.
What were the main characters and images you remember?
Myself, a woman in the background who was just an observer, but could help if necessary, and a baby.
Were any of the dream characters familiar to you?
Only myself.
Did anything in the dream strike you as particularly significant?
My strength, and determination to give birth unaided. The new baby felt very significant.
Where or when was the dream set?
In a dimly lit room. It seemed to be night-time.
How did it make you feel?
Very empowered and joyful. Jubilant!
Your interpretation
In deciding to go freelance, the right choice has been made. I can give birth to the new phase in my life. Help will be there if I need it.

Interpreting your dreams

You can interpret your dreams on several levels. Dreams are usually multi-layered, and when you find the key to the surface meaning of a dream, this can also unlock deeper layers, and enable you to access powerful insights into how your mind works. With practice, you will find that interpretation becomes easier, because you become familiar with the symbols and motifs which your subconscious mind uses to communicate.

Firstly, consider the overview. What is the atmosphere of the dream?

★★

Is it light and happy, loving, comical or threatening? How did you feel on waking? This gives you the general tenor of the dream. Then take yourself through the 'story' of the dream, step by step. Think about the characters: who they are, how they behaved, what they said. Look at each character in the dream as an aspect of yourself, and then relate this to influences, situations or people in your life, and see whether there are any links. Ask yourself whether any of these characters are archetypal. With a fearful dream, think about the message that your Shadow is trying to convey to you. With a luminous dream, ask yourself what is the significance of a message brought by your Essential Self.

The manner in which a dream shifts or progresses is very relevant. Often a dream will suddenly segue into a scenario that appears to have no connection with an earlier section. If so, consider the dream first of all in two parts, and when you have interpreted these separately, look for any common images or messages.

Dreams frequently contain metaphors. For instance, if you dream of a person whom you have never met, see whether you can relate the qualities you associate with this person to qualities within yourself or someone in your acquaintance. If you dream of an ideal lover, you can see this as your Anima/Animus, or view this as a message that you are looking for those qualities in a potential mate, but also contain them within yourself. Perhaps your dream is reminding you of qualities that you are not acknowledging or accepting.

Dreams about famous people, like royalty and film stars, are often connected with archetypes. If you consider the archetypal significance that these characters convey, you may be experiencing a dream of yourself as reluctant hero, saviour, or warrior. Explore how you feel about these elements of yourself, and look at situations in your life where you are currently being pushed to accomplish a difficult task, or to rescue a buried aspect of yourself, or to battle with an unjust situation.

Dreams are sparked by associations, and can be interpreted through practising the art of free association. Often a chance comment will create a flash that brings a previously forgotten dream to full recall. Experiment with associating the symbols in your dreams with events, situations and people in your waking life. Each time you feel a spark that means the association has hit a mark, take that point and see what else you can associate it with. If you dream of being late arriving at a garden party when everyone else is already there, consider what you are worried about completing that is as yet unfinished. Progress your thoughts to your own feelings about timekeeping (are you usually late, or early?), about parties or gatherings of people (do these excite you or make you nervous?), and about gardens (do these convey beauty, relaxation, or the hard work of digging and planting?). Keep the meaning personal to yourself, as well as pondering the traditional interpretation.

Case study

I was with a man who I loved, and who loved me. There were powerful sparks between us – it felt very intense and beautiful. The room we were in was quite dark, and we were standing in front of a large mirror. He was behind me, standing close, and I suddenly felt him go rigid with shock. He stepped back from me, saying 'Your eyes! They've turned red!'

I looked in the mirror, and my eyes were glowing like red coals. I thought at first that it was a trick of the light, and turned my head at different angles. My eyes really were glowing with a fiery red light. He stepped back further, frightened of me, and I turned and moved towards him to put my arms around his neck. I was initially scared of what I'd seen, and of his fear as well, but I told him, 'It's okay. I'm still me.' When I woke up, I felt quite disturbed at first, then strong. I felt I could take care of myself.

To interpret this dream using Level **1**, look at the central motifs of the mirror, the man, and the eyes. Level **2** reveals that the dreamer is in the process of discovering a new and surprising element to her inner nature. Consider the initial atmosphere – total love. The dreamer is with a man with whom she shares intense loving feelings. The mirror is a reflection of herself as others see her. In the 'story' of the dream, this changes swiftly to fear when the man finds that she has an aspect that alarms him. She is shocked, but reassures him. The fiery eyes can be a symbol of demonic qualities, but can also represent the 'fire within', and eyes are the mirror of the soul. She is showing her Deep Self, with all its fire, passion, and molten brilliance, and this intensity can be frightening. Yet she accepted the presence of the power of her inner Self, and calmed and reassured him. She woke up feeling strong and confident.

At the time of this dream, the dreamer, a mature woman, had been experiencing a crisis of confidence in the midst of a difficult situation. The dream signalled to her that she was stronger than she realised, and that she should not be afraid of her inner fire. The man, her Animus, stepped back in the dream, signifying that it was time for her intuition and female instincts to take centre stage.

Requesting dreams

This is an aspect of dream incubation. You can ask for advice, guidance and help before going to sleep, and your dreams can provide answers from the deep well of the subconscious mind. Practising this is empowering, because you are sending signals to your highly suggestible subconscious mind that act as a trigger for creative dreaming. The wisdom-aspect of yourself is given permission to come to the fore and tell you, in symbolic form, what you need to know.

In order for dream incubation to work effectively, you need to feel strongly about the issue or situation about which you are asking. Your skill will develop if you regularly practise recording and interpreting your dreams, because you then become more accustomed to the signs and symbols, and the relevance that these hold for you. You begin to recognise motifs, archetypal resonances, and associations, and can make connections between these and your waking life more easily and skilfully.

To request a dream that will help you to find the answer to a question, first make sure that the issue you wish to explore is clear in your mind. Then write your question down on a piece of paper, three times. This helps to anchor the question in your subconscious. Before you go to bed, put yourself in as relaxed a frame of mind as possible. Put the question out of your mind, and meditate or listen to soothing music for a while. As you prepare to go to sleep, ask the question again, take the piece of paper that you have written it on, place it beneath your pillow, and 'let go' of the question. Try not to think about it. Instead, let your thoughts drift pleasantly as you fall asleep.

On waking the following morning, write down any memories that you have of your dreams, and think about the messages that these contain. Be open to receiving your answer over the next few days; it may not come immediately, but it will usually appear within a week at the most. The more you access this innate ability, the more it will develop, until you can fall asleep after asking your question, and wake with the answer or solution.

Dream Dictionary

Each entry in your dream dictionary is divided into two parts. Use both of these when interpreting your dreams, as this will enable a more in-depth perspective on the messages contained within your dream. The first interpretation describes the surface message that forms part of your dream story. This will help you to interpret the central motifs of your dream.

The second section helps you to understand the hidden symbolism or spiritual significance present within your dreams, often within metaphors. This interpretation lies beneath the immediate surface message of the dream, and it takes more thought to work out its exact meaning in relation to your current situation. You should read this second interpretation after you have thought about the significance of Section 1.

Because dreams are personal creations, they are entirely subjective, and dream motifs can mean different things for different people. These interpretations can only act as a guide for you to unlock the meaning of your dreams. As mentioned in the introduction, the best way to understand and interpret your dreams is to record them, and at the back of this book is a dream diary to help start you off.

A

Abandon

1 Dreaming that you have been abandoned indicates a deep-rooted fear of rejection. You may be worried that someone in your waking life is about to leave. If you dream of abandoning another person, it is likely that you feel reluctantly bound to them.

2 Abandonment dreams can indicate conflict with the spiritual or emotional aspects of yourself. If you have 'let go' of a hope or dream, consider whether you can reconnect with this.

Abyss

1 Dreaming about an abyss indicates that you feel trapped in your current situation. The abyss also indicates fear of the unknown. You may be feeling out of your depth, or are worried about failure.

2 The abyss can represent aspects of yourself that you are afraid of bringing to the surface and would prefer to keep hidden. Entering the abyss can be a journey into the mysteries of the Deep Self.

Accident

1 Dreams about accidents are very common, and reflect feelings of anxiety. They are only very rarely premonitions that you, or someone you know, will have an accident. This dream can mean that you have been bottling up feelings and sense you heading towards a crisis point.

2 Accident dreams can also be a warning from the subconscious to take extra care if you have been in a distracted state of mind.

Actor

1 If you dream that you are an actor, you may be wishing to express aspects of yourself that you do not usually reveal to other people. Seeing yourself under a spotlight means that you hope for recognition, and a more public persona.

2 Actor dreams can mean that you feel that you are feeling pressured by others to put on an act or a role that does not correspond with your own views about yourself .

Afternoon

1 When it is the afternoon in a dream, this indicates long, drawn-out situations. Other people in the dream are those you feel you will be associated with for the long-term.

2 The afternoon is the time of day when you start to unwind from the hectic activity of the morning, and look forward to relaxing in the evening. Whatever plans you are currently making will have positive results, and will be enduring.

Age

1 The age at which you see yourself or a character in a dream can act as a pointer to how you feel about situations in your life. If you dream of a young child, this means that potential is being developed, and will blossom. Dreaming of someone in middle-years shows that events are coming to fruition, and a ripening process is occurring. An old person represents experience that has been gathered, along with maturity and wisdom.
2 The number of an age in a dream can be a significant pointer to that number in your life. Look at what this number represents to you. Age in a dream can indicate your current feelings about your energy level or outlook on life.

Air

1 The quality of air in your dream reflects your feelings about an issue in your life. Crisp, clean air indicates that the situation will soon become clear. Heavy, sultry air reveals that you feel weighed down, and need to rethink your path forward.
2 This dream may be a pun or metaphor. Do you feel stifled, or that you need to 'clear the air' with someone?

Airplane

1 If you are flying in an airplane, this signifies that you are moving swiftly towards the culmination of plans that have been already set in motion. The presence of other people indicates that support is available. Dreams about plane crashes reflect inner anxieties that your efforts will 'crash to the ground'.
2 Because airplanes fly high above the earth, these dreams can symbolise that you are able mentally or emotionally to soar above your current situation, and can look at it from a broader perspective.

Alarm

1 An alarm ringing in your dream can signify 'alarm bells' in your head, and underlying concerns about the wisdom of a current course of action.
2 An alarm can also be a metaphor for a 'wake up' call in your life. This acts as an alert that advises you to view a situation in a clearer light, or to awake to fresh and previously unconsidered possibilities.

Alcohol

1 Dreams in which you are drinking alcohol or are in alcohol-related settings such as a bar serve to remind you to examine any resistance or inhibitions. Observe where and why you are drinking alcohol in the dream, and consider your feelings around this. Now question whether you need to 'loosen up' in any areas of your waking life.
2 Alcohol dreams can indicate that you are having difficulty in expressing your true feelings, and need to find a way to accomplish this.

ALIEN

1 Either being with, or dreaming that you are an alien, shows that you are feeling isolated and alone. This highlights a need to find a way through which you can connect with kindred spirits.

2 Dreams of aliens can reveal hidden fears, especially of the unknown. You may be facing an unfamiliar challenge that makes you nervous. Dreaming that you are an alien can indicate a fear of the unknown within yourself, of repressed aspects of your psyche from which your conscious/waking self has become alienated.

ALLIGATOR

1 As a predatory creature associated with the primitive reptilian brain, an alligator represents deep-rooted fears of losing someone or something dear to you. You may be dealing with feelings of being 'devoured' by a situation.

2 The tough, horny skin of an alligator can be a dream metaphor that indicates that you are being 'thick-skinned', or are feeling aggressive, and need to pay closer attention to the needs of others.

ALONE

1 The environment in which you are alone is significant, and it is important also to reflect on how the dream made you feel on waking. Being alone and happy indicates that you are comfortable with your independence. Being alone in a crowd reflects fears that you do not 'fit in' within your group.

2 Alone also means 'all-one'. This signifies that you need to be more self-sufficient or self-reliant.

AMBULANCE

1 An ambulance dream is similar to an 'alarm' dream, only more urgent. Consider whether your current actions or direction may carry problematic consequences. It can also be related to concerns about your health, or the wellbeing of those around you.

2 Ambulance dreams may be calling attention to important underlying issues that you have been unaware of. The siren and flashing lights of an ambulance are powerful warning signals.

AMPUTATION

1 If you dream that you are having a limb amputated, this symbolises a fear of loss of something or someone whom you feel strongly attached to, and regard as essential to your life.

2 Consider whether you are ignoring an important aspect of your life, and are therefore 'cutting it off'. Amputation dreams can remind you of aspects whose meaning in your life has not been fully recognised. You may also be feeling emotionally or physically 'cut off' from those around you.

A
B
C
D
E
F
G
H
I
J
K
L
M
N
O
P
Q
R
S
T
U
V
W
X
Y
Z

★★★

Amusement park

1 If you dream about an amusement park, reflect on whether you were enjoying yourself, or were nervous of the rides. Amusement park dreams can be a subconscious reminder that you need to create more space in your life for fun and recreation.
2 Dreams featuring an amusement park can signify the need to recapture a sense of childlike enthusiasm and spontaneity. Allow yourself to relax more, and free yourself of limiting inhibitions.

Anchor

1 An anchor indicates the need to be more grounded and 'anchored', and establish a base from which you can work out future strategies. There may be someone in your life who is an anchor, or you may be performing this role for others.
2 Because an anchor is dropped from the air into the sea, and comes to rest in the sea-bed, it can indicate that you are 'tuning in' to your subconscious mind, and are feeling its influence.

Angel

1 Angels symbolise guidance, advice, or help from the Essential Self. Dreaming of angels is a reminder that a higher force is accessible to you, and instructs you that if you ask for help, it will be provided.
2 Because they are spiritual beings, angels represent your desire to connect with the peaceful, loving aspect of the Spiritual Self.

Anger

1 Anger in a dream indicates frustration with an aspect of waking life, either with a situation or a person, which feels safer when released in a dream. Consider who you feel angry with, but cannot express this while awake, or whether you may be the butt of someone else's resentment.
2 As a passionate emotion, anger in a dream can signify that you are repressing your feelings, and need to 'let off steam'.

Animal

1 Animals in dreams symbolise aspects of yourself or others that you need to pay attention to. Consider what is happening with the animal you are dreaming of, and whether it is friendly or threatening. Perhaps it is a familiar animal or a pet? Animals can indicate unexpected allies.
2 Each animal holds a key to human qualities and characteristics. Look at what the animal embodies to you. Animals can also signify hidden desires, or strong feelings about yourself – you may dream of a pig if you have 'pigged out' that day.

A
B
C
D
E
F
G
H
I
J
K
L
M
N
O
P
Q
R
S
T
U
V
W
X
Y
Z

Apartment

1 Unlike a house, an apartment is set out on one level. Dreaming of this means that you are attempting to put your life in order. Consider the size, state, and 'feeling' of the space you find yourself in.

2 Because an apartment is laid out on one floor, you may be feeling that your life is too complicated, and needs to be 'compartmentalised'.

Apparition

1 An apparition in a dream can be an indicator that you are not feeling fully 'present' in an area of your life. You may feel that you are floating through life without making a strong connection with aspects that you previously considered to be important.

2 Apparition dreams can be a warning signal, or even a message from a deceased person whom you have been thinking of, and feel close to.

Apple

1 Dreaming of apples is a sign that your efforts are about to 'bear fruit'. Consider the appearance of the apple. Shiny apples represent good health and fortune. Wizened or rotten apples warn you to choose another course, or to beware of a possible betrayal.

2 Apples can symbolise increasing wisdom and self-knowledge that is shared with others.

April

1 April marks the time of spring when rain fertilises the earth, and growth becomes more abundant. Dreaming that it is April indicates that new plans will lead to success.

2 Reflecting the saying, 'April showers', there may be a mixed time ahead emotionally, since water is connected with powerful emotions, and rain can mean tears. However, this will be viewed as positive in retrospect.

Archway

1 Note the appearance of the archway. A brick or stone archway can signify that you are building a new phase of life for yourself. A floral or leafy archway reveals that soon an offer will be made that will lead to fresh opportunities.

2 Hesitating to pass through an archway means that you are resisting inevitable changes in your life. Happily passing through indicates that you welcome the change.

Arrest

1 If you are arrested in a dream, you are subconsciously dealing with feelings of guilt, or are worried about being 'caught out'. If you arrest another person, then perhaps you need to confront issues around them that disturb you, and talk this through together.

2 An arrest is a way of bringing someone or something to a halt. Consider whether there is something in your life that you wish to bring to an end.

★★

Ashes

1 Ashes, as the remnants of things that have been burned away, can symbolise that you are feeling 'burned out' and depleted. You may have suffered a loss of some kind, or feel that you need to gather your energy and resources in order to stoke up your inner fire.
2 Dreaming of ashes can signify sadness at the ending of a phase or situation in your life. When something 'turns to ashes', this signifies disappointment.

Atlas

1 Dreaming of an atlas means that you are now ready to broach new horizons in your life. An atlas dream can be a prelude to physical travel, either through changing your place of residence, or going away on holiday.
2 Consider which area of the atlas drew your attention. The East symbolises fresh ideas and new beginnings. The South symbolises inspiration and a spiritual journey. The West indicates your emotional life, and the North signifies security.

Attack

1 Attack dreams are manifestations of anxiety. They indicate a sense of vulnerability or powerlessness in waking life. They can also be reflections of hostility that you are subconsciously picking up from someone around you. Ask yourself how you responded to the attack. Did you flee, or fight back? This will give you clues as to how you can empower yourself.
2 If you are the attacker, question whether you feel hostile towards someone whom you consider to be undermining you, and take steps to resolve this.

Attic

1 Dreaming that you are in an attic means that you are taking deliberate steps to build a connection with your Spiritual Self. The levels of a building symbolise the physical, mental and spiritual aspects of yourself.
2 An attic can be a storage space for belongings that are no longer in daily use. You may be dredging up old memories, or need to be reminded of something that you have set aside, that could now be of value to you.

Audience

1 Dreaming that you are in an audience signifies a need to feel part of 'the crowd', and a desire to blend in. If you dream that an audience is watching you, consider how this made you feel. Did you enjoy this, or did it make you nervous or anxious? This reflects your inner feelings about being observed by others, and about 'standing out' from the crowd.
2 You may be conscious of changes to your 'place' in the world. This will lead to increased social standing in the eyes of others.

★★★

August

1 As August is the time of high summer, dreaming of this month means that your life has taken on a summery glow and you may be subconsciously worrying that this period will come to an end.

2 Because August is often a time when holidays are taken, dreaming about this month can indicate a need to take a break from everyday routine, or to temporarily reduce your workload.

Autumn

1 Because harvesting takes place in autumn, dreaming of this season can indicate that ideas or plans are now about to bear fruit. The hard work has been accomplished, and now it is time to reap the rewards and be nourished by them.

2 The seasons in dreams can represent stages of your life. Autumn marks the end of summer, and dreaming of this time can signify that you are leaving behind some of the ideals of your youth, and stepping forwards into maturity.

Avalanche

1 Dreaming of an avalanche can indicate that repressed emotions are having a destructive effect on your life. You may feel blocked by an obstacle that threatens to overwhelm you emotionally and create a 'snowball effect' into more than one area of your life.

2 An avalanche can signify that you fear losing control of your emotions. It is important to find a safe avenue of self-expression and resolution.

Baby

1 Dreaming of a baby does not necessarily mean pregnancy. It signifies new ideas or projects, or a fresh start in your life, that can grow and develop with careful nurturing.
2 Baby dreams may also indicate a longing for a state of innocence and purity, and a desire to be cared for or looked after by others. If you are taking on extra responsibilities, ensure that you take time to nurture yourself.

Back

1 Your backbone is what holds you upright. Dreaming of your back can signify that you need extra strength, support or courage in order to win through in a situation. Seeing someone else's back can indicate disapproval, or fear of being ignored.
2 Turning your back symbolises the rejection of a situation, whereas 'backing off' or 'backing down' indicates that you feel overwhelmed, and need some space.

Baggage

1 Dreaming of baggage indicates that you feel weighed down by emotions associated with events in the past. Observe whether you are carrying your baggage willingly, or are trying to offload it. This reflects how you are dealing with these feelings.
2 If you are reluctantly carrying someone else's baggage, consider whether you are allowing other people to offload their 'stuff' onto you, to your detriment. Happily carrying another person's baggage indicates that you wish to be helpful.

Balcony

1 Dreaming that you are on a balcony represents a need for more control over your life. There may be a longing for prestige or recognition. Balcony dreams can signify that you are ready to 'go public' over a situation.
2 What you see from the balcony is significant. If you see animals, this signifies that you are gaining control over urges or desires. Seeing children represents a need to be more playful and spontaneous.

Balloon

1 Because they are associated with parties, balloons in a dream mean that you are connecting with your childlike, playful self. Take this as a message to explore your sense of celebration and fun.
2 If you are floating with a balloon, this indicates a sense of pleasure and well-being. If balloons are popping in dream, you are afraid that the 'bubble will burst', leading to disappointment.

★★★

Bank

1 If you dream that you are entering a bank, this indicates that you need to pay extra attention to managing your resources, both physical and financial. Being inside a bank vault can mean that you are currently feeling a need for increased security in your life.
2 Dreams involving a bank robbery symbolise that your energy or resources are depleted, or that events you have been awaiting are being 'held up'.

Baptism

1 The connotation of baptism is that of washing away past thoughts, deeds and actions. Dreaming of this indicates that you are starting afresh on a new phase of your life. You may be undergoing major changes that fill you with a sense of renewal.
2 Baptism dreams can mean that you feel cleansed of a difficult situation from the past. Let go of any sensations of guilt or regret that are holding you back from true healing.

Basement

1 Dreaming that you are in a basement indicates that you are having to deal with suppressed memories that make you uncomfortable.
2 Basement dreams relate to the subconscious mind and hidden emotions. Pay attention to the 'story' within the dream to shed light on the message from your subconsicous.

Bath

1 Dreams set in the bathroom mean that you are longing for more privacy in your life. As the bathroom is a place of peace and seclusion, you may be feeling that too many demands are being made on your time and energy.
2 A bath represents emotional and spiritual cleansing, and a need to unwind and immerse yourself in the luxury of self-indulgence.

Battle

1 Dreams involving battles indicate that you are dealing with conflict, or are struggling with a decision. Consider how many people are engaged in the battle, and whether you are in a position of strength or weakness. Are you fighting a losing or winning battle?
2 If you view people in the battle as being different aspects of yourself, you may be experiencing a conflict between, for example, your head and your heart.

Beach

1 Dreaming of a beach indicates that you are searching for new horizons in your life. You may be in need of some peace and tranquillity, or a break from routine.
2 A beach can represent the borderline between your conscious and subconscious mind. You may be experiencing insights that arise from deep within yourself, and enable you to view life from a new perspective.

A B C D E F G H I J K L M N O P Q R S T U V W X Y Z

★★★★★★★★★★★★★★★★★★★★★★★★★★★★★★★★★★★★

Bed

1 If you dream of being in bed, this means that you need to take 'time out' to consider your needs. Perhaps you are conscious of a lack of privacy or peaceful rest.
2 Bed is where you sleep and dream, but it also represents the sensual aspect of yourself. Is the bed large or small, neat or rumpled, comfortable or uncomfortable? Your feelings about your sexual life are related to your impressions in the dream.

Beggar

1 If you dream that you are begging, this reflects a fear of 'not having enough', or a concern about a depletion of your resources. Are you afraid of losing your job or home, or someone who is a source of emotional sustenance?
2 Dreaming that you are giving to a beggar indicates that you will receive help when you most need it. Support is at hand.

Bell

1 Dreams featuring a bell have similar connotations to those about an alarm. You need to pay heed to any warning signals that your subconscious mind is sending you.
2 Bells in dreams can signify celebration if they are wedding or other joyful bells. This means that your venture will be successful.

Bicycle

1 A bicycle dream reflects a desire to recapture the freedom from responsibility and restraints that you experienced during childhood. If you see yourself cycling happily, you will be able to release current tensions by opening up to a more receptive frame of mind.
2 Bicycles can symbolise your journey through life. If the bicycle is in good order, you feel confident about the direction you are taking. If the bicycle is old or rickety, this reflects worries about your ability to attain goals.

Bird

1 Dreaming of birds signifies a sense of freedom, and flight from cares and worries. Birds also symbolise the Spiritual Self. Consider whether the birds are caged or flying free. This shows how you are feeling about your life at a deep level.
2 The type of bird in your dream is significant. A bird of prey indicates seeing an overview. Vultures signify a fear of loss. A bird's nest represents wealth.

Birth

1 Dreaming about giving birth signifies that a new idea or project will meet with success, especially if this is connected with your creativity. You may be in the process of discovering new gifts or talents that will be beneficial to you.
2 Birth dreams can symbolise the discovery of new aspects of yourself. You may be 'giving birth' to previously unrecognised elements within yourself.

A B C D E F G H I J K L M N O P Q R S T U V W X Y Z

Blessing

1 If you dream that someone is bestowing a blessing on you, this signifies that you will receive a favour or a gift that will take on a spiritual connotation.

2 Dreams in which you are giving a blessing indicate that you are growing into your inner sense of self-empowerment.

Blindfold

1 Being blindfolded in a dream symbolises anxieties over not being able to see a clear way forward. You may feel that someone you know is trying to deceive you, or is deliberately hiding something important from you.

2 If you are blindfolding someone else in a dream, this means that you are nervous that they will find out something about you that you would prefer to remain hidden.

Blindness

1 A dream in which you are blind can mean that you are 'blinding yourself' to something that you should be paying attention to. Perhaps you are ignoring your own faults, or someone else's, or are afraid to learn an uncomfortable truth.

2 Without the sense of sight, other senses become sharper. By allowing these to take precedence, you may experience a 'blinding revelation' that truly opens your eyes.

Blood

1 Dreams in which you, or someone else, are bleeding, signify that you are concerned over health, and about losing something that you associate with life-force or life-blood. Injury in a dream often reflects real or imagined slights that 'cut you to the quick'.

2 The blood in your veins carries life-giving oxygen and nutrients. Dreaming of blood-loss means that you are feeling stifled and powerless in an area of your life.

Blue

1 The predominance of the colour blue in a dream symbolises your sense of connection with your spiritual self. By considering what is blue in your dream – the sky, the sea, a flower – you can relate this to your inner feelings. Being surrounded by blue sky represents a sense of freedom and joyous liberation.

2 Blue dreams can also be viewed as metaphors. Perhaps you are 'feeling blue', or are concerned that your wish will only be granted in a 'blue moon'.

Boat

1 Boats in a dream signify the vehicle transporting you through life. Observe the state of the boat. Is it battered, or ship-shape? This reflects how you feel about your body.

2 If a boat is drifting away from you, you may be feeling that you have 'missed the boat' and let an opportunity pass. If a boat is moving towards you, good luck is on its way, as your boat is 'coming in'.

A
B
C
D
E
F
G
H
I
J
K
L
M
N
O
P
Q
R
S
T
U
V
W
X
Y
Z

★★

Body

1 The meaning of your dream depends upon which part of the body you are dreaming of. The head indicates concerns about decisions. Chest problems mean that you are feeling suffocated by a situation. Your hands represent a need to create and direct your life. Your legs indicate a desire to walk towards or away from a situation.
2 The body in dreams is connected with your Ego, your sense of self in relationship to the world around you. Consider whether you feel in control of your body, or whether it has a 'mind of its own'.

Book

1 Dreaming about a book signifies that you are ready to receive new knowledge or information. If the book is old, you will receive advice from an older person whose wisdom you respect. A new book indicates fresh understanding. The subject of the book is important. Consider whether it is a spiritual text, a poetry book, or a comedy, and apply this to your life.
2 Books can symbolise spiritual openess, since you may feel you can read people 'like a book', or that your life is 'an open book'.

Bouquet

1 A bouquet of flowers in a dream is a symbol of happiness and congratulations. If you receive a bouquet, this denotes that you wish to be recognised and applauded for your achievements. If you are giving a bouquet, you wish to acknowledge and state your feelings for the person in receipt of the gift.
2 A bouquet can represent a gathering of people who are special to you.

Box

1 Dreaming of a box signifies that you are feeling 'boxed in', or confined. You may be resentful of limitations that are imposed on you by the expectations of others. If you are opening a box, this indicates that you are willing to explore deep emotions or issues. Closing a box signifies 'putting a lid' on some aspect of your life.
2 An ornate box, or jewellery box, can mean that you wish to keep your treasures, your inner feelings, closed away from prying eyes.

Breast

1 Dreaming of breasts symbolises that you are feeling in need of nurturing. In dreams, breasts tend to be connected with nourishment and mothering rather than with attraction or sexuality.
2 The state of health of the breast is significant. A wizened or diseased breast reflects inner concerns about your health, and a lack of self-care. A full breast indicates that your needs will be met.

Bride

1 Dreaming of a bride indicates good fortune and happiness. This may be connected with a creative or business partnership, as well as having an association with marriage. If you are the bride, this means happiness with family and friends. If you are watching a wedding, you may be invited to a gathering or celebration.
2 A bride can also symbolise the sacred marriage between the Anima and Animus, the female and male aspects of the self, leading to an increased sense of wholeness.

Bridge

1 Dreams featuring a bridge signify a transition between one stage of life and another. If the bridge is rickety and you are afraid of falling, you are nervous of the changes to come. If the bridge is strong, you can meet new experiences with confidence.
2 A bridge is also a symbol of the connection between the ordinary and the Spiritual Self. Crossing a luminous bridge indicates a strong emerging spiritual connection.

Briefcase

1 To dream that you are carrying a briefcase indicates that you are focusing strongly on your career. A locked briefcase signifies that you feel 'shut out', or are concerned about a promotion or change that is due. An open briefcase indicates that an offer will be made to you.
2 Dreams featuring a briefcase can be a reflection of your feelings about confinement and conventionality.

Brother

1 Dreaming of a brother can be an indicator of rivalry, protection, or vulnerability in your waking life, depending on the age of your dream brother. An older brother in your dream may signify a figure of authority in your waking life. A younger brother may reflect an urge to protect a younger male friend or colleague.
2 As a metaphor, a 'brother' dream can represent your feelings about a group, or brotherhood, in your waking life.

Building

1 If you dream that you are building something, you are taking steps to create something new in your life, through the power of your own efforts. It also signifies a need for independence, and a sense of pride in your accomplishments.
2 Seeing buildings in a dream can reflect your feelings about aspects of your life. Consider whether the building is small or large, a cottage or a cathedral, and what these represent to you. If the building is familiar, what feelings does it inspire in you?

A
B
C
D
E
F
G
H
I
J
K
L
M
N
O
P
Q
R
S
T
U
V
W
X
Y
Z

★★★★★★★★★★★★★★★★★★★★★★★★★★★★★★★★★★★★★★

Burglary

1 You may be anxious about your safety, or your security in the home or at work. Consider whether you disturb the burglar in the act, or frighten him/her away. This reflects your inner views on your ability to cope with insecurity.
2 Another aspect of a burglar dream is connected with your sense of self. You may be feeling that someone is depriving you of your self-esteem, or robbing you of rightful praise or recognition.

Burial

1 You may be feeling 'buried' beneath cares, responsibilities, or pressure of work. Or that you are unable to express yourself adequately because the needs of others are more pressing or demanding. Do you feel that others have forgotten you?
2 Burial dreams can indicate buried or suppressed emotions that are too painful to face or deal with in waking life.

Bus

1 Dreaming of a bus indicates your feelings about your journey through life, and about those who accompany you on that journey. You may be wishing for more company, or to become involved with a community.
2 If you are driving the bus, you feel in control of your life, and are in a position to guide, or take charge of others.

Butterfly

1 Dreams about butterflies signify a desire to be more light-hearted, to take life less seriously. Alternatively, the dream may be pointing out that you are not focusing clearly enough on projects or goals that are important to your future – that your 'butterfly mind' is too busy flitting from one thing to another to settle down and tackle the task at hand.
2 Butterflies symbolise transformation. The metamorphosis from a caterpillar to a butterfly represents a rebirth process and a blossoming occurring in your life.

Cage

1 Dreaming of a cage signifies that you feel trapped, or deprived of an element of your personal freedom. Consider whether you are inside or outside the cage.

2 A cage also represents a sense of being controlled by someone or something. This could even be elements of yourself, such as fears or doubts that are holding you back. If you see a key to the cage in your dream, the way out is within your power.

Cake

1 A cake represents the good things in life, through its association with celebrations. Dreaming of a cake indicates that you need to focus more fully on the positive aspects of your life, and refuse to be dragged down by negativity.

2 Do you want to 'have your cake and eat it'? Or are you anticipating news that will be 'the icing on the cake'? The 'story' within your dream will help you to decipher which meaning is appropriate for you.

Cancer

1 Dreams in which you, or someone you know, have cancer are usually anxiety dreams. This rarely means that you are seriously ill, but it can be a message from your subconscious mind that you should be taking better care of your health.

2 Cancer dreams can signify that your physical, emotional or mental resources are at a low ebb. You may be feeling overwhelmed, yet reluctant to 'let go' and allow inner healing from past traumas to take place.

Candles

1 Candles can represent your current energy levels. If the candles are glowing brightly, this indicates that your willpower and confidence are strong. Guttering or extinguished candles represent low physical energy or depression. Depending on the condition of the candles, you may be feeling 'sparked up' or 'burned out'.

2 Candles represent brightness, hope and guidance. Dreaming of a mass of lit candles indicates a strong connection with your Spiritual Self.

Canal

1 As a man-made route for travel, dreaming of a canal indicates that you have clearly mapped out your journey through life, and are determined to stick to this.

2 The association with water means that canal dreams are connected with the channelling of your emotions. Consider whether you are allowing yourself enough emotional spontaneity or flexibility.

★★★★★★★★★★★★★★★★★★★★★★★★★★★★★★★★★★★★★★★

Canoe

1 Dreaming that you are paddling a canoe symbolises that you are confident about being in control of your life. Consider whether you are alone or unaccompanied, as this reveals whether you are relying on another person to help you.

2 The conditions in the water that you are negotiating inform you of your feelings about current events. If the water is calm, you sense the way ahead is clear. Turbulent water indicates that you fear losing control, and are anticipating problems.

Car

1 Dreams of cars reflect your feelings of control, and your self-motivation. Consider whether you are driving the car, and are therefore in control of your life; or whether you are a passenger, and are letting someone else 'take the wheel'.

2 The conditions in which you are driving are relevant, and reflect your feelings about your life. Is the road smooth and straight, or full of hairpin bends? This reveals whether you are in the 'driving seat', or are acting recklessly or carelessly.

Carousel

1 Dreaming that you are riding on a carousel signifies that you fear you are trapped on a 'merry-go-round', with no immediate end to your current situation. You may be feeling, 'Stop the world, I want to get off'.

2 Consider whether you feel that events are spiralling out of control. A 'stuck' situation within a relationship or work issue can be resolved by stepping off the carousel and making a much-needed decision.

Castle

1 A castle symbolises power, security, authority and protection. If you dream that you are in a castle, you could be in need of a safe haven where you can take time out from everyday concerns.

2 There may be a strong subconscious longing to be viewed as important or special, to be a 'king' or 'queen' who is set apart from the crowd. If the castle is surrounded by clouds, as in a 'castle in the air,' this warns you that you are fantasising, and should pay attention to reality.

Cat

1 Cat dreams can carry several connotations. Consider whether this is a cat or a kitten, and is friendly or hostile. Cats signify a desire for independence and autonomy, and a strong connection with the intuition. A kitten signifies a need for playfulness.

2 If a cat is approaching you in a friendly manner, this represents good fortune to come. A hostile cat is a warning that someone you know is not to be trusted.

★★

Cauldron

1 Dreaming of a cauldron symbolises an attunement to your feminine power, because of its association with goddesses and witches. You feel empowered in your waking life and you are on the threshold of wisdom and regeneration.
2 The 'cauldron of plenty' of pagan traditions carries a connection with the Arthurian Grail. Cauldron dreams can indicate that you are being nourished by your spirituality, and will not need to worry about going 'hungry' or unfulfilled.

Cave

1 If you dream that you are in a cave, this signifies that you must confront the obstacles you face by 'digging deep', and searching for the root cause.
2 A cave can indicate that information that has been buried in the subconscious mind is coming to the surface. It also relates to a womb-like space, where fertility and creativity emerges from silence. Meditation or temporary solitude, as in 'going into your cave', will be helpful.

Chase

1 Being chased is one of the most common dream themes, especially in times of stress. It indicates that you are trying to run away from a difficult situation. If you are chasing someone, you are fearful that something may be taken from you.
2 Consider the elements in the dream. If you are being chased by a stranger, your own subconscious fears are catching up with you. If the pursuer is someone you know, you may be feeling that others are 'chasing you', and expecting too much of you.

Children

1 Dreams about children can signify a need to connect with your inner child; the innocent, playful aspect of yourself. You may be longing to return to a time in the past when life seemed more simple and straightforward.
2 Children in dreams symbolise aspects of yourself that are as yet undeveloped, and are calling out for your attention. You may be feeling vulnerable or insecure. The message in these dreams is often that you need to examine issues that should be given more consideration. Children also represent new ideas.

Chocolate

1 Dreaming of chocolate signifies that you have been suppressing desires, and need to loosen up and indulge yourself a little.
2 Chocolate dreams may indicate a craving for something that you consider to be forbidden or out of reach. The sensual appeal of chocolate can symbolise that you have been denying a longing for love and comfort.

★★★★★★★★★★★★★★★★★★★★★★★★★★★★★★★★★★★★★★

Church

1 A church is a place of sanctuary, where all who enter are temporarily set apart from everyday cares and strife. You may be feeling 'put-upon' or stressed, and should consider the possibility of taking a well-earned break.
2 There is a spiritual connotation to church dreams. Your subconscious mind is prompting you to search for answers to important questions that can be a guiding light in your life.

Circle

1 Consider whether you are inside or outside the circle in your dream. If you are inside a circle, this indicates a sense of self-containment and fulfilment. Being outside a circle means that you are 'circling around' a situation or issue. It can mean that you are 'going round in circles', and cannot find a clear resolution.
2 Symbolically, circles represent wholeness, protection, and a sense of connection with the Eternal Self. You may benefit from creating a 'sacred space' within your home, where you can relax and connect with your Spiritual Self.

Classroom

1 Classroom dreams are 'big' dreams that serve to remind you that you are embarking on a powerful learning curve in your life.
2 Consider who is in the classroom, and how you feel about being in this environment. Are you studying, or resisting being there, or simply passing through? Your answers to these questions reflect your feelings about a current learning situation.

Cliff

1 Dreaming you are on the edge of a cliff represents a fear of failure, or of the unknown. Consider whether you are standing at the edge, or are falling. Standing on a cliff means a choice needs to be made. Falling symbolises that you fear losing control.
2 Cliff dreams are messages that important decisions need to be made, and that there is an element of risk involved. Through 'taking the leap,' your life will be changed in far-reaching ways.

Clock

1 Clocks signify a need to pay attention to how you are coping with issues that revolve around the passage of time. Note whether the clock is running fast or slow. The message can be that 'time is running out,' and you need to act speedily on a decision. Or you may be setting yourself unreasonable deadlines.
2 Consider the details of the dream, and what they mean to you. Are you aware that your 'body clock' is ticking? Perhaps you have been more aware of your age lately, and have been thinking about starting a family, or pursuing a goal.

Closet

1 Dreaming of a closet indicates that you fear that uncomfortable secrets will be revealed – concerning either yourself, or someone you know.
2 You may be feeling reluctant to disclose personal information to others and are holding yourself back from experiencing intimacy by 'closing yourself off.'

Clouds

1 Clouds in dreams usually represent a lack of clarity, and can be a signal that your judgement or view of a situation is 'cloudy'. If the clouds are grey or dark-coloured, and especially if they are storm clouds, you are suppressing feelings of anger.
2 White fluffy clouds floating in a blue sky represent the connection with the spirit, especially if you wake feeling on 'cloud nine.'

Coffin

1 Dreaming of a coffin signifies that a situation or person is confining you, and 'putting a lid' on your ideas or suggestions. If you are inside a coffin, you need to resolve a situation that is 'closing in' on you.
2 Because of its connection with death, a coffin in a dream can indicate that a phase of your life is about to come to an end. Even if you do not recognise this consciously, your subconscious is telling you to move on.

College

1 As with dreams of classrooms, a college represents a learning situation. However, the lessons in this case are intellectual rather than emotional.
2 Dreaming of a college indicates that hard work and perseverance will bring rewards and recognition. You may be offered a promotion on the strength of your achievements or dedication.

Corpse

1 Seeing yourself as a corpse in a dream indicates a time of great change, such as changing your residence or job, or leaving behind a relationship. If the corpse is not your own, someone close to you may be undergoing a transformation in their lives.
2 Dreaming of a corpse of the opposite sex can mean that you are shutting off aspects of yourself that reside within the Anima or Animus. Consider whether you are ignoring aspects of yourself to the detriment of your sense of wholeness.

Crash

1 As in 'alarm' dreams, crashes are a wake-up call from your subconscious that warn you to pay attention to a situation in your waking life.
2 A crash dream can have a positive meaning. It can signify that something surprising and noteworthy is about to happen.

★★★

Cream

1 Dreaming about cream is a good omen. If you are eating or drinking cream, this signifies that good fortune, increased prosperity, or a promotion are on their way.
2 You may be feeling like 'the cat that got the cream'. You are being rewarded for something that you have striven for, and your life is about to take a turn for the better.

Creek

1 A creek signifies a short journey and fresh experiences. If others are also present in your dream, these experiences will be shared.
2 Consider the terrain around the creek, and the water in it. If the water is muddy, you may currently be feeling as if you are 'up the creek without a paddle.' There are likely to be delays and some frustration before you can move forward.

Cross/crucifix

1 Because of its association with the Christian religion, a cross in a dream can represent pain and suffering that will ultimately lead to transformation. Is there a 'cross you have to bear?'
2 A cross in a dream can represent the triumph of the mind and spirit over adversity. Its original symbolism is the unification of mind/spirit and body/matter.

Crossroads

1 Dreaming that you are standing at a crossroads is a message from your subconscious mind that it is time to make a choice, and to act decisively.
2 Note the direction you are facing in, as this could help resolve your confusion. East means you should start afresh. South advises you to follow your dream. West indicates listening to your emotions. North tells you to withdraw.

Crown

1 A crown represents status and recognition. You will receive praise for a task that you have accomplished, or a goal you have met.
2 Your subconscious mind is reminding you to look at the achievements in your life, and congratulate yourself on those. If you have been feeling discouraged, ask yourself what you consider to be your 'crowning glory', and acknowledge this.

Crystal

1 If you see a clear crystal in a dream, this indicates that a state of clarity will emerge from confusion. If the crystal is cracked or broken, you may be challenged by a crisis of confidence that could hold you back from reaching for your goal.
2 Conside the type of crystal you see in your dream. A clear quartz indicates spiritual insights. A rose quartz symbolises love. A black onyx reminds you that you are protected. An amethyst represents tranquillity.

A B C D E F G H I J K L M N O P Q R S T U V W X Y Z

Dam

1 Dreaming about a dam represents the suppression of strong emotions. If you are building a dam, you are attempting to prevent your feelings from breaking through and overwhelming you. If you are knocking down a dam, this means that your subconscious mind is telling you that it is time to 'let it all out'.

2 Consider what else in your life appears to be 'dammed up' at the moment. You may be feeling stifled, and held back from expressing your full potential.

Dancing

1 If you are dancing in a dream, this indicates a need to express yourself more fluidly, and reminds you to look at what is joyful in your life. Consider whether you are dancing alone, or with other people. Dancing alone means that you can take pleasure in your personal achievements. Dancing with others represents the integration of various elements of yourself, along with a feeling of 'belonging' in a group.

2 The type of dancing that you are experiencing is relevant. If you are dancing slowly, this indicates a sensual attraction. Fast dancing reminds you to loosen up inhibitions. Ballet or more disciplined dancing signifies a need for more structure as well as joy in your life.

Danger

1 Dreams involving danger are most common during times of stress and anxiety. The dangers that you are dealing with can often be a subconscious reflection of how you perceive the cause of your anxiety. If you are tackling a fire, this means that the situation involves 'inflammatory' issues. Floods or rapids signify overwhelming emotions and a fear of losing control.

2 Consider how you are dealing with the danger in your dream. If you are facing it, your subconscious is telling you to battle on. If you are escaping, this can be a message to step back or retreat.

Darkness

1 Dreaming of darkness indicates an attunement with the unconscious. Firstly consider how you feel about the darkness in your dream. If you are afraid, this signifies deep-rooted fears, possibly concerning death or endings. If you feel comfortable in the darkness, you are currently in need of privacy and extra space.

2 Because darkness signifies an absence of light, you may be feeling 'in the dark' about something that needs to be uncovered or discussed. Consider whether you feel shut out in any way.

★★

DAWN

1 Seeing the day break in a dream implies that a situation that has been difficult or unclear is about to improve and 'brighten.'
2 Dawn can signify the beginning of a new phase in your life. Opportunities may be offered to you that will lead to a positive change.

DECEMBER

1 Dreaming about December indicates that you need to find a guiding light that can illuminate a difficult situation. The connection with the shortest days of the year signifies that you feel pressured that there is 'not enough time' for your endeavours.
2 December is a month of celebration, and after the Winter Solstice the days begin to lengthen, so dreaming of this month can mean there is 'light at the end of the tunnel.'

DEATH

1 Death dreams rarely mean that you are going to die. They can be a subconscious message telling you to break free of a situation. If you dream that someone you know has died, this means that they are undergoing a major upheaval, and need support.
2 A death dream can wake you up to a fresh awareness of a relationship or situation, and inform you that 'the life has gone out of it'. You may need to consider moving on, and starting anew.

DESCENDING

1 Dreams in which you are descending may be reflecting subconscious worries that you are not making forward progress. It can indicate that matters seem to be 'sliding downhill', and that you have been losing hope over a situation.
2 Descent dreams can symbolise that you are now ready to 'go deeper', to delve into difficult memories in order to generate healing and attain a deeper self-understanding.

DESERT

1 Dreaming that you are in a desert can indicate feelings of loneliness or isolation, and a need for nurturing. A recent emotional or material loss may be preying on your mind. If you can see an oasis, a state of regeneration is approaching.
2 The desert can also be a place of spiritual illumination, because the lack of stimulation puts you closely in touch with the wisdom of the Essential Self.

DEVIL

1 Seeing a devil in a dream indicates that your Shadow aspect has a powerful message for you. You may be grappling with feelings of guilt, or have been under pressure to act against your better judgement.
2 Devil dreams often mean that your fears are coming to the surface. Worries about material possessions, or an unhealthy emotional obsession may be indicated.

Diamonds

1 Your personal interpretation of diamonds is relevant when they appear in a dream. Consider whether you view diamonds as a status symbol, a romantic commitment or declaration of enduring love, or a sign of victory. If you are being given diamonds, something that will be very precious to you is on its way.
2 Diamonds are formed deep within the earth, from carbon that has been compressed under great pressure. You may be feeling the strain of pressures from work or relationships, but your subconscious is reminding you that great gifts will emerge from this difficult time.

Digging

1 Firstly consider whether you are digging something up, or digging in order to bury something. If you are unearthing an object, this means that hidden information is about to come to light. If you are burying an object, you are afraid of revealing either your true feelings, or some other aspect of yourself.
2 You may be given information about the past which will have great relevance to you in the period to come.

Dinosaur

1 Because dinosaurs symbolise the far-distant past that is difficult to access, dreaming of them indicates that you are struggling with belief systems that strike you as being extinct, or outdated and of no current use. A 'dinosaur' figure in your life may be trying to make you conform to something that you do not agree with or believe in.
2 You may be held back by deeply engrained beliefs that were instilled in you during childhood. Dinosaur dreams can be reminders to leave the past behind.

Dirt

1 If you dream of dirt, this means that you wish to 'wash your hands' of something that you find distasteful or demeaning. Someone close to you may be trying to draw you into gossip, or 'dishing the dirt' on you.
2 Consider whether you have been feeling particularly negative about a person or situation. Dirt dreams can signify that negativity is preventing you from seeing clearly.

Disguise

1 If you are in disguise in a dream, consider what you are wearing, and what this represents. If the dream is set in a masked ball, you are hiding aspects of yourself from others in order to feel accepted. If you are running away in disguise, you are fearful of others discovering your motivations. A jester or clown disguise shows that you are hiding sadness beneath a layer of levity.
2 Disguise dreams can indicate a desire to hold back your emotions by attempting to hide them from those around you.

★★★

Diving

1 Dreams in which you are diving represent the exploration of areas of your subconscious mind. You may be considering investigating systems that involve an understanding of symbolism. Diving dreams signify an urge to delve beneath surface matters, in order to develop a deeper understanding.

2 Consider your feelings while you were diving. Did you feel joyous, excited or anxious? Your reaction informs you of your true feelings about uncovering deeply hidden memories or information.

Divorce

1 On a literal level, if you are married or cohabiting, divorce dreams can mean that you are insecure in your relationship. If you are single, dreaming of divorce indicates that an important situation in your life is coming to an end.

2 Dreams of divorce can also relate to the separation of aspects of yourself. You may be shutting off elements of your personality in order to focus on developing other areas at their expense. Divorce dreams remind you that integration is needed.

Doctor

1 Dreaming of a doctor signifies a healing process that is taking place at a deep level. These dreams are a reminder that help can come from within yourself if only you open yourself to it.

2 Consider whether a situation in your life is in need of healing. As a doctor represents conventional medicine, healing can come through traditional methods. If the doctor is a surgeon, healing will come through 'cutting away' from the problem.

Dog

1 A dog in a dream represents close friendships. If the dog is friendly, you can trust those around you, and can be assured of their faithfulness and loyalty. A hostile dog indicates that someone around you does not have your best interests at heart.

2 Because dogs are sociable creatures, dreaming of them can signify that you need to make more of an effort to connect with other people. A barking dog can be a 'wake up' call, to alert you either to danger or to new possibilities, depending on your feelings in the dream.

Dolphin

1 Because of their permanent smile and playfulness, dolphins in dreams indicate a need to reconnect with the joyful, fun-loving aspects of yourself. Make a note to take life less seriously, and to be more sociable.

2 As they live in the sea and yet breathe air, dolphins represent a bridge between the subconscious and conscious mind. Your subconscious is communicating an important message to you about allowing a deeper connection with the people around you.

Door

1 Dreaming of a door indicates that an area of your life is either opening up before you, if the door is open, or is about to be closed off if the door is shut.
2 Consider what the door is made from. Wooden doors signify a barrier that could be overcome, with effort. A metal door is a clear message that an avenue you have been exploring is unlikely to be viable.

Dove

1 Dreaming of doves indicates that a troubled situation will be brought to a peaceful conclusion. Doves symbolise happiness in love and relationships.
2 A white dove can symbolise an increasing connection with the spiritual aspect of yourself. You may have been feeling contented and 'at peace' with yourself recently.

Dragon

1 If you dream of a dragon, first consider your feelings during the dream. Were you afraid, or accepting? Dragons represent sexual energy and your sense of personal empowerment. If the dragon is fearsome, you are nervous about the intensity of your feelings. If you are in control in the dream, you can deal with a strong attraction without feeling overwhelmed by it.
2 A dragon can also represent elements of yourself that you are striving to suppress in order to appear less intimidating to other people.

Drinking

1 Dreaming that you are drinking has a similar meaning to 'alcohol' dreams. You may be taking life too seriously, and this is a message to relax and unwind more, and release some inhibitions.
2 Drinking dreams can also indicate an urge to 'drink more deeply' of life. You may have been feeling on the periphery rather than a full participant. Take this dream as a message to engage yourself more fully.

Driving

1 There are close similarities between 'car' dreams and 'driving' dreams, as both of these signify taking control of your life. Dreaming that you are driving indicates that you are purposefully directing your life with a specific aim or goal in mind. Consider whether you are driving slowly, which means that you are prepared for the 'long haul', or are speeding, which indicates a willingness to take risks in order to attain your goal more quickly.
2 The type of vehicle that you are driving is important. A sports car denotes a desire for speed and status. A battered old car denotes a determination to make the journey in any available manner. A truck indicates your willingness to 'bulldoze' your way through obstacles.

★★★★★★★★★★★★★★★★★★★★★★★★★★★★★★★★★★★★★★

Drought

1 Dreams of drought carry a similar connotation to 'desert' dreams. If you are with other people, there is a need to deal with an issue that is 'drying up' communication with someone. If you are alone, you may be feeling that opportunities are 'drying up' or coming to nothing.

2 Drought dreams signify a sense of emotional barrenness or lifelessness. You may be feeling drained or 'sucked dry' through giving too much of yourself to others. There is a need to replenish your energy reserves.

Drowning

1 To dream that you are drowning is a sign of great stress, and a message from your subconscious to take care and slow down. It signifies that you are feeling totally overwhelmed and helpless in the face of too much pressure.

2 Drowning dreams, because of the connection between water and the emotions, can mean that you have not been openly acknowledging feelings of suffocation. Other people are leaning on you too heavily, and the dream is a clear message to step back.

Drum

1 Hearing drumming indicates an attunement to the rhythms in your life. If you are the drummer, you are calling up new aspects and rhythms in yourself that will open up fresh areas of exploration.

2 There is a connection between the drum and the heartbeat. You may need to listen to what your heart is telling you. Drum dreams can also symbolise 'drumming up' new ideas, business or friendships.

Dusk

1 Dreaming that it is dusk signifies the ending of a situation, and a lack of clarity around how to proceed to the next stage or phase.

2 As the transition between day and night, dusk dreams can also represent a connection between your logical, waking self, and your intuitive, dreaming self.

Dying

1 Dreaming that you are dying signifies that you are approaching the end of a highly charged emotional situation. Dreaming that someone you know is dying means that there could be a parting of the ways.

2 You may be aware that closure is needed around an issue that you have been dealing with. Dreaming of dying is a message from your subconscious to let go, and to channel your energy in a different direction.

Eagle

1 The eagle, with its strength and clear vision, symbolises freedom, authority and nobility. Dreaming about an eagle means that you are now ready to view the whole picture of your life, rather than allowing yourself to be bogged down by minor details. Your willpower and perception are strong, and you are gaining in confidence.
2 In native traditions, the eagle represents a connection with the realms of the Spirit, and is a reminder to broaden your horizons.

Ear

1 Dreams where details of ears are revealed are a clear message to be careful about what you say. These are also a reminder that you should be listening more closely to what other people are trying to tell you. Consider whether you have been 'deaf' to a plea for help, or need to keep an ear open for opportunities.
2 A focus on ears in a dream can be a subtle subconscious message that tells you to listen to your body. You may have been overstretching yourself, or ignoring your body's signals about nutrition or rest.

Early

1 If you are early in a dream, you may be anxious about tasks that need to be done in your waking life. Consider whether you are waiting for someone to arrive, or for something to happen, and take into account your feelings in the dream.
2 As with the saying, 'the early bird catches the worm', the message from your subconsious reminds you that new endeavours will be successful if you prepare for them carefully and give them plenty of time to develop.

Earth

1 If you dream about earth, you are being reminded to 'ground' yourself, to search for ways in which to increase your stability, or to build solidly upon prospects that are being explored. Consider whether the earth is wet or dry, solid or boggy, as this indicates how you perceive your current position. Muddy earth represents a lack of firm foundations or clarity. Dry or hard-packed earth symbolises a secure basis that you can build upon.
2 Earth can relate to 'Mother Earth', and the fecund aspect of yourself, because of its association with growth and nurturing. Your creative or practical projects are likely to be successful.

Earthquake

1 Dreams of earthquakes occur most often when there is anxiety in waking life over a sudden threat to your stability. You may be worried about a change in your circumstances, either financial or in a relationship.
2 Tumultuous emotions can cause earthquake dreams. You may be feeling that the 'rug has been pulled out from under your feet', leaving you without solid ground to stand upon. You may have been feeling a overwhelming sexual attraction recently which has precipitated an earthquake dream, as in 'the earth moved'.

Eating

1 If you are eating in a dream, this can signify a craving for love or affection. If you are being eaten, you should focus on what is 'eating' at you, disturbing your equilibrium in waking life.
2 Eating dreams can be a signal to nourish yourself spiritually and psychologically, as well as physically and emotionally.

Eclipse

1 Observe whether it is the sun or the moon that is eclipsed in your dream. You may be over-compensating in one area to the detriment of another. If the moon is eclipsed, you are blotting out your psychic or sensitive side. If the sun is eclipsed, you are closing off your logical, reasoning aspect.
2 If you dream of an eclipse, your attention is being drawn to a matter that has been temporarily set aside in favour of something else. Consider what has been left undone. Question whether you are feeling 'eclipsed' by someone, and are living in their shadow. Eclipse dreams can mean that you are unable to allow your true self to shine.

Ectasy

1 Dreaming that you are in a state of ecstasy is a sign that good news is about to arrive. A new friendship or love affair could be imminent and this will bring you joy.
2 Feelings of ecstasy in a dream can also signify a strengthening connection with your Essential Self, which inhabits a state of bliss. You may be experiencing a sense of attunement in your waking life that will lead you to feel part of the 'whole'.

Eel

1 Dreaming of an eel can have sexual connotations. If the eel is moving towards you, a strong attraction is about to enter your life. If the eel is moving away, you are attempting to deny an attraction that you consider to be inappropriate or unsuitable.
2 Consider whether you are misplacing your trust in someone around you. If an eel slips from your fingers during your dream, somebody (a slippery character) may be withholding information from you.

Egg

1 Dreaming about an egg signifies potential and new beginnings. An egg denotes a new cycle of life about to begin, and a birth, either physical or symbolic. Because the egg symbolises a gestation period, you need to be patient while events develop. Broken eggs signify dreams that have been prevented from coming to fruition.
2 Eggs also denote a sense of wholeness. Dreams of eggs can symbolise an understanding of your potential, and a determination to fulfil this.

Elephant

1 If you dream of an elephant, ideas that may seem 'big', or even grandiose, will come to fruition. Elephants symbolise wealth and longevity. You are willing to move gradually but inexorably towards your goal, and no obstacles will be big enough to hold you back.
2 Because elephants are renowned for their long memories, your subconscious mind may be signalling that you need to remember what is most important to you. The devotion between pairs of elephants signifies that a current relationship is strong.

Elevator

1 If you dream of a rising elevator, this indicates promotion or recognition. You are 'going up' in the world. If the elevator is falling, you are anxious about losing your job, prestige, or status. A elevator that has broken down signifies that you feel 'stuck' in your current situation.
2 Elevator dreams can be a connection with the unconscious. Consider your feelings in the dream, and whether you were alone or in company. The people with you can be viewed as aspects of yourself that need attention or recognition.

Elopement

1 If you are eloping in a dream, you are afraid of losing the respect or friendship of someone close. If a partner is eloping, this reflects your fears of losing him or her.
2 Consider whether there is something or someone in your life that you feel a need to distance yourself from. What is making you want to run away? You may be reluctant to face an aspect of yourself that is making you uncomfortable.

Engagement

1 At a literal level, dreams of engagement signify a desire for commitment, either within a love relationship, a business partnership, or a venture. Engagement dreams can also remind you to connect more fully with an aspect of your life; to 'engage yourself', rather than daydreaming.
2 Engagement dreams can also symbolise a realisation of the close connections between your body, emotions, mind and spirit. You may be receiving a reminder that your mental state affects your feelings and your physical health.

★★★★★★★★★★★★★★★★★★★★★★★★★★★★★★★★★★★★★★

Enticement

1 Dreams of enticement indicate that a seductive or tempting influence in your life may, if you succumb to it, lead you into trouble. Or it can mean that this area of yourself is being suppressed.

2 If you dream of being enticed, you may be giving too much energy to logical thought processes, and are ignoring your feelings. Your subconscious mind may be reminding you that pleasure is a necessary aspect of life.

Entrance

1 Dreaming of an entrance indicates that a new path is opening up before you, and that it is important for you to pursue this. Opportunities may come from an unexpected source.

2 An entrance in a dream can signify the development of previously hidden talents. Pay attention to synchronicities or coincidences, and experiment with new ideas, even if these do not initially appear to 'make sense'.

Envy

1 If you feel envy in a dream, this means that you are conscious of a sense of something lacking in your waking life. If you are the person who is the target of envy, someone close to you may not be as well-disposed towards you as they pretend to be.

2 Envy dreams can be a signal that you need to open yourself to a deeper exploration of your potential. There may be an awareness of a need to connect with a 'missing link' within yourself, in order to attain an increased sense of wholeness.

Epaulets

1 To dream of epaulets signifies a dropping-off in your social life. It can also point to an association with someone that will lead to uncomfortable gossip and could damage your reputation.

2 Because epaulets denote rank or status, you are subconsciously yearning for recognition from others. Your subconscious mind is reminding you that to earn recognition, you must first acknowledge your own strong qualities.

Erotica

1 Erotic dreams can be the result of unfulfilled desires or yearnings, or can arise through highly charged emotions. You may be denying yourself pleasures in life, or suppressing your appetites in other ways as well as sexually.

2 Eroticism in dreams can be a reminder that you have been too busy focusing on the needs or wishes of others, and need to pay attention to your own needs – whether this is through relationships, eating well, relaxing more, or treating yourself. The focus on self-centred pleasure in erotic dreams is a message to put yourself first for a change.

Escape

1 Dreams in which you are escaping are pointers towards aspects of your waking life that are unsatisfactory. Question what it is that you wish to run away from. Are you avoiding something unpleasant or uncomfortable? You may be afraid of dealing with a person or an issue, or are feeling overburdened. The other components in the dream will help to clarify this.
2 Escape dreams can indicate that you are refusing to face up to an aspect of your own nature. You may have been acting out of character, or feel that you have been unreasonable in waking life.

Establishment

1 Dreaming of an establishment signifies a need for stability, reason, and conformity. It can also indicate, depending upon your feelings within the dream, a rebellion against the status quo. Consider the nature of the establishment. A hospital signifies help and healing. A prison indicates that you feel stifled or hemmed-in.
2 The various archetypes that form your internal make-up can be viewed as an establishment, each ruling its own section of the psyche. You may need to be more aware of integrating these aspects, in order to feel more comfortable with yourself.

Evasion

1 Evasion dreams indicate a reluctance to face the truth. If you are evasive, this symbolises fears that others are unwilling to accept the 'real' you. If someone is evading you, this is a warning that undercurrents are present in your relationship.
2 Evasion dreams can be a reminder that you are refusing to recognise an aspect of yourself. It is necessary to be truthful with yourself about your inner motivations.

Evening

1 As with 'dusk' dreams, the evening signifies an ending to a situation or set of circumstances. If stars are shining there will be cause for hope, even if you are about to give up. A view of the moon can mean that you need to examine emotional undertones, and adopt a different perspective.
2 Consider the events during the dream, and how you feel. Evening can be a time of rest and relaxation after the day's work, and this can be a reminder to slow down and allow yourself more leisure time.

Evergreen

1 To dream of an evergreen can indicate that a situation in your waking life has the potential to be long-lasting and stable. Evergreens can represent prosperity.
2 The sense of continuity that is symbolised by evergreens implies that you have found your 'place', or sense of 'rightness' in the world. This indicates a growing sense of maturity and accomplishment.

★★★

EVIL-DOER

1 If you are the evil-doer in the dream, this means that you have been struggling with feelings of resentment, or with urges that make you uncomfortable in waking life. If someone else is the evil-doer, this represents a fear that you may have wronged them.
2 The actions in the dream will clarify your true inner feelings about suppressed fears or unacknowledged anger.

EXAMINATION

1 Dreams of sitting an examination are often connected with stress and anxiety, with feelings of not being 'good enough', or fears that you are being tested beyond your limits. You may be feeling a need to live up to others' expectations of you.
2 Examination dreams can be a message to 'examine' your true thoughts and feelings around an issue, and to follow what feels right, rather than what is expected of you.

EXPLOSION

1 An explosion in a dream is your subconscious' way of releasing charges of pent-up emotions. Explosion dreams can be triggered by upheaval in waking life, and can 'clear the air' for resolution.
2 Consider all of the elements and motifs within the dream. Explosion dreams can be a major wake-up call, bringing your attention to feelings or reactions that you have been suppressing or denying. Often these dreams can bring about important insights on awakening.

EXECUTION

1 Who is being executed in your dream? If you are the victim, this indicates a realisation that you are in a treacherous situation that could lead to loss. Perhaps you are concerned about 'losing your head', by surrendering to an urge to speak your mind. If you are the executioner, you are subconsciously aware that something needs to be removed from your life.
2 To execute also means to 'carry out'. You may have been avoiding necessary action, and your subconscious mind is insisting that it is time to make a move.

EYE

1 Because eyes are our instrument of vision, dreaming of eyes implies that there is a need to 'look carefully' and 'see clearly' in a current situation. Open eyes indicate a willingness to face issues. Closed eyes signify a reluctance to face the truth.
2 The eyes are the windows to the soul. Dreaming of eyes is a reminder that you cannot hide from yourself, and that a part of you is an eternal witness. Eyes can also mean the 'I', the Self. Consider the expression in the eyes. Eye dreams can also indicate the presence of a guardian spirit that 'watches over' you.

Face

1 If you see the faces of strangers in your dream, this indicates that you are curious to find out more about the people around you. An old face can represent the accumulation of wisdom or sage advice. A youthful face can mean that you need to reconnect with childlike elements within yourself.

2 Faces in dreams can represent different aspects of yourself. Featureless faces can be unnerving, but this means that an aspect of yourself is being hidden. Ask yourself what you are unable or unwilling to 'face'? You may be avoiding 'facing up' to a situation that has been worrying you.

Falling

1 Dreams in which you are falling are a more extreme manifestation of 'descending' dreams. Ask yourself how you felt while you were falling, and whether the sensation was pleasurable or frightening. Falling dreams can indicate a fear of failure, of 'falling short', or of loss of control. You may need to ground yourself, to take care and make yourself more secure.

2 You may be weighed down by extra burdens or responsibilities. Look for metaphors in your dream. If a dream includes falling leaves, a phase of your life could be coming to an end, and a new beginning ready to unfold.

Family

1 Family members in dreams can represent elements of yourself. To dream of the mother signifies a need for nurturing. The father implies responsibility or authority. Siblings indicate shared tasks or interests.

2 Dreams of your family can be a reflection of attitudes towards outside relationships. Consider which family member is most prominent in the dream, as this will indicate your subconscious feelings about current relationships in your life.

Farm

1 Dreaming of a farm can signify a longing for a simpler, more basic way of life. Note the landscape, and any animals that are present, as these can give messages about how to reduce stress in your life.

2 Farm dreams can remind you to plant the seeds of new ideas, and nurture them to fruition. They can indicate a need to plough your imagination in order to find the answers to questions that you have been asking.

Fat

1 If you dream of fat, you may be experiencing concerns about your body, and how other people view you. If you are embarking on a new diet or a health regime, 'fat' dreams remind you to pay attention to your own feelings, rather than taking the opinions of other people on board.
2 Fat dreams can be a symbol of nurturing, wealth, and prosperity, as in 'fat of the land'. They can indicate coming success.

Father

1 Dreams about your father, or a father-figure, indicate the need to access the power principle within yourself. You may be wanting to be looked after, or are dealing with issues around authority – either your own authority, or that of someone else. The attitude of the father in your dream will inform you about your own inner feelings.
2 Father dreams can be reflections of your subconscious feelings about relationships with male figures in your life.

Fear

1 Fear can manifest in many ways through dreams. The feeling of fear in a dream is usually a reflection of inner fears that are being thrust to the surface. Observe the object or source of your fear, and how you dealt with this during your dream, as this can give clues as to how to deal with your fears in waking life.
2 Fear in dreams can be related to feelings of helplessness, or a loss of self-empowerment. From a spiritual perspective, fear indicates a fruitless attempt to hold onto illusions.

Feather

1 Dreaming of feathers indicates that current anxieties or worries are going to be less of a concern than you anticipated. A 'feather in your cap' signifies achievement and success. A 'feathered nest' symbolises wealth.
2 Floating feathers represent a lightness of being that is gathered from your Spiritual Self. A gift of a feather, or a bunch of feathers, symbolises long-lasting friendship.

February

1 If it is February in a dream, this signifies that you are concerned about your health or relationships, or feel 'left out in the cold'. Consider the elements and motifs in the dream for extra clues as to its significance.
2 Because the first spring flowers begin to emerge in February, dreaming of this month can represent a sense of renewal, and increased energy or production after a difficult time.

FEMALE

1 Female figures in your dreams represent an aspect of yourself. Consider the appearance and behaviour of the female. If she is bold, provocative or assertive, you need to work with these qualities. If she is gentle or maternal, this reminds you to tap into this aspect of yourself.
2 For a man, an unfamiliar female in a dream represents the Anima, his female counterpart. For either sex, female dreams indicate a need to listen to the intuition, and to acknowledge feelings.

FENCE

1 Fences represent boundaries in dreams. You may be feeling a need for solitude, or to create firmer boundaries. Consider where you are placed in the dream. Are you 'fenced out', or 'fenced in'? If you are fenced out, this indicates concerns about being excluded. If you are fenced in, you may be feeling trapped. If you are 'on the fence', you are having difficulty in making a decision.
2 Because fences are man-made barriers, you could be deliberately closing yourself off from becoming too intimate with others.

FEVER

1 If you are suffering from a fever in a dream, you feel overwhelmed by obstacles, and are finding it difficult to put up resistance to fight your way through. If you are tending someone who has a fever, you need to nurture an aspect of yourself that has been weakened by stress or criticism.
2 Dreams of a fever can indicate intense feelings that you are unable to express.

FIELD

1 Dreaming of green fields indicates new opportunities coming your way. If the fields are barren or brown, you need to find a way in which to recover flagging motivation. Fields of grain represent fertility and prosperity.
2 Fields can represent your creative impulses, and the fertility of your mind. If the fields are small, or hemmed in, you are feeling creatively constricted. Large, lush fields represent new horizons.

FIGHTING

1 If you dream that you are fighting, consider the position you are in. Did you win, or lose? Observe who or what you are fighting with in the dream, and whether this takes the form of a play-fight or a battle.
2 The conflict inherent in fight dreams can be traced back to inner battles between warring elements of yourself. Perhaps you feel torn between two elements in your psychological make-up. Identifying these can help you find a peaceful resolution.

A B C D E F G H I J K L M N O P Q R S T U V W X Y Z

★★

Finding

1 Dreams about finding are a sign that something new is coming into your life. The nature of the found object or person will inform you about this fresh influence.
2 If you dream of finding something precious or surprising, this represents an important discovery about yourself that could prove to be revelatory.

Fire

1 Dreams of fire hold several meanings, depending upon the nature of the fire, and your feelings in the dream. Fire can signify illumination after a dark time, or warmth and friendship, passion, purification, destruction, or good fortune.
2 Observe your feelings and actions in the dream. This will reveal whether you are 'on fire' with excitement, elation, or desire, or are 'fired up' with enthusiasm or anger. If you are too close to the flames, you may be afraid of 'getting burned'.

Fire-fighting

1 If you dream that you are fighting a fire, this indicates that you are battling with a situation that has become heated or inflammatory.
2 Fire-fighting can represent an inner urge to 'dampen down' over-enthusiasm or passion. This can indicate a fear of strong emotions.

Fireworks

1 Dreams of fireworks are release dreams, which allow intense emotions to be safely activated or dissipated. Fireworks in a dream can also signify a cause for celebration.
2 Repressed or suppressed feelings can set off firework dreams. This can open up the conscious mind to seek out solutions to inner conflicts. There may be a strong attraction that you are nervous of acting on.

Fish

1 As fish symbolise the watery element within the subconscious mind, dreaming of fish represents how you deal with deep emotions. Fish dreams can be reminding you to 'go with the flow'. A fish on dry land means that you may be feeling like a 'fish out of water', and are uncomfortable about sensations of not belonging in a crowd.
2 Dreaming of fish can symbolise a spiritual quest that involves exploring areas of the mind that lie beneath the surface.

Flag

1 If you are waving a flag in your dream, this indicates a desire to make your views public. If it is rolled up, this indicates that you keep your views secret.
2 Note the colours of the flag, in order to decipher the nature of the dream's message. A red flag indicates anger or courage. A white flag symbolises retreat. A black flag represents sadness, or grief. The flag of a country can mean travel.

A B C D E F G H I J K L M N O P Q R S T U V W X Y Z

Floating

1 Dreams in which you are floating symbolise a need to connect with levity, and to relax more. Floating dreams tend to include feelings of happiness or inner peace, and signify that although there is work to be done, success will come. If you are uncomfortable about floating in your dream, you may be concerned that you are drifting through life, or within a situation.
2 Floating dreams can symbolise a connection with the Essential Self, through a sensation of 'flying free' or 'floating on air'.

Flood

1 Dreaming of a flood indicates that a situation has become out of control. Because of the connection between water and the emotions, flood dreams imply that you are feeling overwhelmed, and at the mercy of a 'rising tide' of emotion.
2 Another aspect of flood dreams is the indication that your personal feelings are 'flooding out' into areas of your life, such as career, which are inappropriate. This could be a warning to find safe channels through which to direct your emotions.

Floor

1 A floor in your dreams represents your grounding – the foundation that you rest on, and that you base your belief-systems upon. If the floor is clean and shiny, your feelings and motivations are clear. A muddy or grimy floor signifies lack of judgement, or lack of clarity or direction.
2 Consider how you were feeling before you fell asleep. Have you been 'floored' by surprising news? If the floor is made of stone, you may fear that a situation has reached 'rock bottom'.

Flower

1 Fresh flowers in dreams signify harmony, love and friendship. The type of flowers will offer more information. Roses symbolise love. Peonies represent passion; lilies can mean the ending of a situation. If the flowers are withered or dying, you are afraid that a friendship is coming to an end.
2 Flowers can represent the blossoming of your Inner Self. If you see petals opening, this indicates new horizons and opportunities that will lead to fulfilment.

Flying

1 Flying dreams have many interpretations. First consider your feelings during the dream. If you were 'flying free', this indicates release from stress or pressure. Dipping and diving represents an urge to show off accomplishments. 'Flying high' can mean promotion. Note whether you are alone, or in company.
2 Dreams of flying also symbolise liberation from physical cares or restrictions, and the flight of the soul that is untouched by worldly considerations.

★★

Fog

1 Dreaming of fog indicates a lack of clarity, or a loss of direction in waking life. This can also represent a sense of obliqueness, in which you are aware that something is being kept hidden from you.

2 Fog in dreams can relate to your perception. There may be too many choices for you to see clearly, and to find out which path is best for you.

Food

1 Food in dreams symbolises nourishment and nurturing. It can represent active thinking processes, as in 'food for thought', or it can symbolise sharing, loving and giving, and abundance.

2 Food can symbolise spiritual nourishment. Consider what the food is. A feast can signify that all of your needs are met. A scanty meal can indicate that you need to find ways in which to nourish yourself on all levels.

Foot

1 Your feet represent your manner of locomotion through life, and your feelings about the direction your life is taking. If your feet are firmly on the ground, you are anchored and secure. If you are running, you are in a hurry to achieve your aims. Walking steadily indicates determination.

2 The feet are associated with the Spiritual Self, and the manner in which you walk your spiritual path.

Forest

1 If you dream of a forest, this indicates a desire to move deeper into the mysteries of the unconscious mind. Forest dreams can also signify a desire to step away from everyday life, to retreat into peace and solitude. A thick, green forest can symbolise coming abundance. A dark forest can represent fears of losing your way on life's path.

2 As a place of retreat and quietude, dreaming of a forest signifies a need to take time out in order to be alone for a while. Perhaps you have not been able to see 'the wood for the trees', and need to step back and see things in perspective.

Fountain

1 Dreaming of a fountain means that you are becoming aware of your connection with the source of spontaneity and playfulness within yourself. A clear fountain signifies fulfilment, nurturing, and a sense of attunement to the inner sacred.

2 Dreams of a fountain relate to your emotions and the unconscious mind, so the state of the water flow can indicate your level of inner vitality. Observe whether the water is sparkling or muddy, free-flowing or sluggish.

Fox

1 Dreaming of a fox symbolises craftiness or cunning. You may be concerned that someone is deceiving you. Or you could have intentionally or unintentionally misled someone, and are facing the consequences within yourself.
2 Foxes in dreams can represent a resurgence of the sensual aspects of yourself. You may be feeling 'foxy', and desire to reveal this to others.

Fragrance

1 Dream fragrances can be haunting, and even though the fragrance itself is often forgotten on waking, the feeling that this engenders can remain. Floral fragrances signify love, friendship, and acceptance. Harsh or unpleasant fragrances are a warning that something is going wrong. Sharp, citrus fragrances are a 'wake up' call.
2 Often fragrances appear in dreams about deceased relatives or friends. This can be a 'signature scent', and is a sign of comfort that tells you to let go of your grief.

Friends

1 If you dream of friends, consider the atmosphere of your dream. A group of welcoming friends indicates a celebration to come. A friend whose back is turned signifies tensions that need to be resolved.
2 If the friends in your dream are gathered around you, this symbolises that you are in tune with the various aspects of your nature, and can be 'friends' with yourself.

Frog

1 Dreaming of frogs can be a reminder to look beneath surface appearances, as in the story of the frog that turned into a prince. Frogs can signify an improvement in your health and wellbeing.
2 Because frogs transform from tadpoles, and can move between the water and the land, they can signify a major change in consciousness, and a 'leap forward'.

Frost

1 Dreaming of frost can indicate a 'chilly' atmosphere between yourself and someone else. It can also mean that a situation or project is temporarily frozen, or 'on ice', and that the only course of action is to wait for it to thaw before moving forward.
2 You may have been closing down your emotions recently, or 'freezing out' others.

Funeral

1 Funerals in dreams symbolise a transition phase, during which you need to come to terms with loss or disappointment. Consider whether you are alone or supported.
2 Dreams of funerals can occur when you have been faced with the 'death' of a dream, or an aspect of yourself such as naiveté or innocence. These dreams are the mind's way of acknowledging this, and providing release.

★★

G

Gale

1 If you dream that you are caught in a gale, this can mean that you have been 'blown away' by recent events that you feel are beyond your control, and are struggling to keep your feet on the ground. Changes are imminent and may be disruptive, but you will have to hold on to your equilibrium.

2 Dreams of gales signify that you have suffered a recent upheaval, whether emotional or financial. As winds belong to the element of air, which rules communication, it is important to take steps to resolve arguments or differences of opinion. Wind can symbolise a particularly passionate part of ourselves.

Gambling

1 Dreaming that you are gambling indicates that you need to 'take a chance' in a situation that involves some risk. If you are watching others gambling, but are not participating, this implies a fear of taking unnecessary risks.

2 Consider whether you are currently gambling with something important in your life. Gambling dreams can be a message from your subconsious mind that you are not paying close enough attention to a situation that that may seem minor, but that could lead to the loss of a relationship.

Game

1 If you dream that you are playing a game, this indicates a need to break away from your usual approach to a situation, and look for an element of fun or play, rather than taking things too seriously. If you are with others, observe whether you feel part of the game, or excluded.

2 Game dreams are related to how you play the game of life. Are you playing to win, or just enjoying the process? Consider whether you are following rules, or are prepared to be a maverick. Strategy games indicate that a logical approach is important to you.

Garage

1 A garage is the 'home' for vehicles that represent your manner of moving through life. If the garage is empty, this signifies that you are experiencing a loss of direction. Several vehicles in the garage indicate a choice as to your way forward.

2 Garage dreams are related to your inner motivation and 'drive'. Consider whether the garage is clear or cluttered, oily or clean, as this indicates what needs to be looked at or done in order to spur you on.

A B C D E F G H I J K L M N O P Q R S T U V W X Y Z

GARBAGE

1 If you dream about garbage, this is a message that it is time to throw out any old, outworn or useless ideas that are cluttering up your head-space. You may be clinging to outdated ideas or presumptions.
2 The elements and motifs within your dream provide clues as to what needs to be discarded. If you are throwing away clothes, this indicates a change of image, and a rethink about how you present yourself to the world. Discarding food signifies that you should let go of a situation or relationship that no longer nourishes you.

GARDEN

1 Dreaming of a garden indicates a need for more beauty, growth and creativity in your life. If you are tending the garden, you are taking steps to create fertile ground for new ideas or projects.
2 A garden represents your inner life. Consider what you are doing in the garden. If you are relaxing, you are comfortable with yourself. If you are pruning or weeding, it is time to do the same with aspects of your life.

GARRET

1 Dreaming of a garret, the very top space of a building, implies fresh ideas and creative impulses. If you dream of living in a garret, you wish to step away from conformity, and go your own way.
2 As each level of a building is related to an element of yourself, the garret signifies your rational thinking processes. You may need to take some time out in order to formulate plans, as these will prove to be successful if you focus on them.

GATE

1 A gate, like a doorway, signifies a movement from one stage of life to another. If the gate is open, this indicates opportunities opening up for you. If the gate is closed, you are in danger of missing an opportunity for growth. Passing through a gateway indicates a transition time that will lead to change.
2 Consider whether you are alone at the gate, or whether there is a gate-keeper whom you must pass. If so, this means that something within you is holding back, and it is important that you examine this, and give yourself permission to move on.

GHOST

1 Dreaming of a ghost can mean that you are in a state of confusion, or that you are concerned that the solution to a problem appears to be eluding you. If the ghost is a person you know, your relationship with them needs to be clarified.
2 As characters in your dreams can be interpreted as aspects of yourself, ghosts can be old memories or emotions that are returning to 'haunt' you. Or you may be feeling ignored or not 'seen' by those around you.

★★★

Giant

1 If you dream of a giant, first consider your feelings in the dream. If you are afraid, this means that you are feeling overwhelmed by a situation or responsibility that seems too 'big' to cope with. If the giant is friendly, you are prepared to take on more in order to achieve your aims.
2 A giant can represent the strong, powerful aspect of yourself. It indicates that you feel confident about facing challenges. If the giant is among normal people, this means that success and recognition will come your way.

Gift

1 If you dream that you are bestowing a gift, this means that you are willing to give of yourself emotionally to others. If you dream of receiving a gift, this indicates that something good is about to come your way from an unexpected source.
2 A gift in a dream can mean that you are opening up emotionally and spiritually, and are entering a higher state of awareness about yourself and your purpose in life.

Giving birth

1 Dreaming that you are giving birth does not necessarily mean that you are going to have a real baby. As with 'birth' dreams, this indicates that something new is about to enter your life.
2 Giving birth in a dream also relates to discovering hidden talents or gifts. If you give birth easily, your way forward will be smooth. If the birth is difficult, you will have to work hard to attain your goal.

Glass

1 Dreaming of panes of glass means that there is a barrier between you and your goal. If the glass is transparent, this means that you can see your way through to a solution. If the glass is cloudy, there are undercurrents that need to be recognised before you can move ahead.
2 Glass in a dream indicates that you feel shut out or cut off from those around you, and need to find an avenue of communication that will open up a clear way forward.

Glasses

1 Dreaming that you are wearing glasses indicates that you wish to see a situation more clearly. If the glasses have tinted lenses, observe the colour of the tint. Pink lenses indicate a desire to see good in a situation. Blue lenses represent an increasingly spiritual outlook. Sunglasses mean that you are emotionally secretive and wish to avoid revealing too much about yourself.
2 If the glasses are cracked or askew, this means that your view of a situation has been shattered, and needs to be dramatically altered before you can find a resolution.

Gloves

1 Gloves create a barrier to your feeling nature. You may be sensing a need to protect yourself, or intuitively know that careful handling is needed at this time. Dreaming that you receive gloves as a gift can signal a new relationship which you may initially view with caution.

2 Dreaming of gloves can mean that you need to become more assertive, as others are not considering your feelings. It can also reveal that you are wary of displaying any vulnerability, even to yourself.

Goat

1 Goats in a dream can symbolise your earthy, sexual side, and remind you that you can display this. You may be embarking on a new and passionate love affair.

2 The ability of goats to climb to inaccessible places, and to reach the pinnacle of mountains, indicates that your ambition and determination are strong, and that you will achieve your aims, even if this takes time.

Goblet

1 A goblet is a powerful feminine symbol that is associated with the womb and the waters of life. Dreaming of a goblet indicates shared emotions, and the ability to 'drink deep' of life. If you dream that you are sharing the goblet with another person, this signifies a commitment in a relationship.

2 Because of its association with the chalice and Grail, a goblet in a dream can represent abundance, nurturing, and a state of spiritual union.

God

1 Dreaming of a visitation of a God-like figure means that you are aiming high, and are reaching for success that, although considered unattainable to others, will become a reality for you. A message from a God figure in a dream can inform you of how to move forward in your life.

2 As an aspect of yourself, a God figure in dreams symbolises advice or guidance from your Higher Self or Essential Self.

Gold

1 If you dream of gold coins, artefacts or jewellery, this indicates coming wealth, and an improvement in your health. If the gold objects are ancient, this can mean an inheritance. Shiny new objects indicate that prosperity will come through your own efforts.

2 Dreaming that you are surrounded by gold light means that you are spiritually protected, and that others view you as wise, and will come to you for advice or healing.

★★★★★★★★★★★★★★★★★★★★★★★★★★★★★★★★★★★★★

Goose

1 Dreaming of a flock of geese signifies an urge to be assertive, and to protect yourself from any who wish to intrude on your privacy. If the goose is in an oven, you may be concerned that you have 'cooked your goose', and have made life difficult for yourself.
2 As with the 'goose that laid a golden egg', this dream can represent the emergence of gifts from within yourself, that will lead you onto a new and abundant life-path.

Grandparents

1 Dreaming of your grandparents symbolises that you are surrounded by support for your endeavours, and that others will help you to achieve your aims.
2 Grandparents in a dream also symbolise the wise aspect of yourself. A grandmother figure indicates the need to nurture and accept yourself; to recognise your qualities and help them endure. A grandfather figure signifies knowledge and benevolence.

Grass

1 If you are surrounded by lush green grass, this indicates coming fertility and abundance, especially if the grass is on your property in the dream. Brown or dead grass reminds you that your plans will only succeed if you 'water' them by putting the strength of your emotions into them. If the grass belongs to a neighbour, you may be feeling that 'the grass is greener', and that others have the good fortune you desire.
2 Grass in dreams symbolises your feelings about your personal growth. If the grass is healthy, you are satisfied with your life. If the grass is wild, long or full of weeds, you may need to 'cut back' strong feelings that are hindering you.

Grave

1 Dreams that involve graves have strong connections to 'death' dreams. They suggest that it is time to bury an issue, and move on. Grave dreams can be a metaphor for how you view a current situation. A 'grave' issue may be worrying you intensely.
2 Your subconscious mind could be telling you that you need to 'kill off' a negative habit or train of thought that is causing you emotional damage. If you see a name on a gravestone, consider which character traits you specifically associate with that name, and observe these within yourself.

Green

1 A profusion of green colours in a dream signifies abundance and harmony. Consider the nature of any objects that are coloured green. A green item of clothing can mean that you are opening up to new methods of self-expression. Seeing green objects in your dream can indicate a time of prosperity and creativity to come.
2 Green in dreams is a sign that healing is taking place at a deep inner level, and that this will spill out into external areas of your life.

Grey

1 Grey shades in a dream are a subconscious reminder that you need to take a current situation or issue seriously.
2 Dreaming in grey tones indicates that you are feeling depressed or drained, and need to search for an element that can bring 'colour' and positive feelings back into your life.

Groom

1 Dreaming of a bridegroom symbolises an urge for commitment, whether this is within a relationship, a business venture, or to yourself. You may need to 'groom' yourself in order to be at your best, mentally and physically, for a particular situation.
2 For a woman, dreaming of a groom can symbolise the Animus, her male counterpart. Consider the action that is taking place within the dream, and view this as advice on how to proceed.

Guitar

1 Consider whether you are playing the guitar, or are in the audience. Dreaming that you are making music on a guitar signifies a need to embrace life more fully. If you are listening to the music, the category that the music falls into denotes what you can add to your life. Classical music signifies increased relaxation and harmony. Flamenco music indicates a need for more passion in your life.
2 Dreams of guitars can be a reminder to 'tune into' your creative side, and to ensure that you express this more fully.

Gun

1 Dreaming of guns indicates suppressed aggression. If you are holding or firing a gun, you are feeling a need to express yourself in a powerful manner, to 'shoot off' your feelings and be certain that others listen to you. If a gun is pointing at you, this signifies that you feel threatened by a person or situation.
2 As guns represent enforced control and domination through fear or aggression, you may be battling with an aspect of yourself that is dominating your thoughts.

Gypsy

1 Dreams of gypsies indicate that you wish to break away from convention, and to experience increased freedom and autonomy. Gypsies in dreams can also represent a feeling of alienation from those around you.
2 The connection with the gypsy lifestyle, which consists of change and movement, symbolises a subconscious urge to move on from a constricting situation, and to express yourself more freely.

Hail

1 If you dream that you are caught in a hailstorm, this indicates a feeling of being battered and overwhelmed by negative thoughts and emotions. You may be feeling 'flattened' by a situation that has shocked and dismayed you deeply.
2 As hail is composed of drops of frozen water, dreaming of hail can indicate that you need to find a safe way in which to express feelings of unhappiness, rather than damage yourself by keeping your feelings 'frozen' or locked away.

Hair

1 Hair in dreams signifies your feelings about your vitality, sexuality, and powers of attraction. Dreaming that your hair is shiny and healthy indicates recovery after a period of ill-health, or a positive turn in the area of your love-life. Dreams that your hair is falling out warn you to take better care of yourself. If your hair is tangled this signifies confusion.
2 Hair also represents your conscious thoughts, motivations and ideas. Brushing or combing your hair indicates that you are paying attention to your thoughts, and acting on those.

Hall

1 Dreams of a hallway indicate a time of change and transition. You may be feeling that you are moving into a new phase, but are not yet sure what this will consist of. Consider whether there are doors in the hall, and whether these are open or closed, as this will reveal clues as to what is in store for you.
2 If the hall is dark and gloomy, this signifies that you are concerned about the steps you have been considering taking. If the hall is light, bright and airy this denotes a positive attitude towards the future.

Hammer

1 The use to which the hammer is put in your dream will help you to understand the dream's meaning. Firstly question whether you have suffered a 'hammer blow' or shock recently. If you are wielding a hammer in order to piece something together, this suggests a need to mend broken relationships. If the hammer is being used to destroy something, you may need to examine and break down a habit, attitude or train of thought that is destructive for you.
2 Because a hammer signifies the use of force in which to create change, dreaming of a hammer can remind you to act swiftly and decisively.

Hand

1 The action that the hands are engaged in during your dream will reveal its meaning. Clasped hands indicate friendships or partnerships. Praying hands symbolise a need to connect more with the spiritual aspect. A shaken fist signifies anger or aggression. Outstretched hands mean that you are inwardly crying out for help.
2 Look for metaphors in your dream. Something may be 'close at hand'; you may be reminding yourself to 'lend a hand', or someone you know may be acting in an 'underhand' manner.

Handcuffs

1 Handcuffs in dreams signify restraint and constraint. You may be feeling curtailed or 'policed' in your waking life, or forced to follow rules and regulations that you do not agree with, but are stuck with.
2 If you are dealing with issues of control, either your own or another person's, this can manifest as handcuffs in a dream. Observe who is in charge, and who is being handcuffed, and relate this to aspects of yourself.

Happiness

1 Dreaming that you are happy signifies, literally, that happiness is on its way into your life. If you dream of making others happy this indicates a willingness to give of yourself.
2 Intense feelings of happiness can be experienced in dreams, to the extent of being woken by your own laughter. This signifies a close connection with the blissful state of your spiritual nature.

Harming others

1 Dreaming that you are harming other people is an indicator of suppressed feelings of anger or frustration. The manner in which you harm in your dream relates to the manifestation of your inner feelings. Using a weapon indicates a desire to make your feelings known forcefully. Using your hands signifies that you need to communicate your feelings.
2 Since all of the dream characters are aspects of yourself, you are subconsciously harming, or causing problems, for yourself. What does the person being harmed symbolise to you as an element of your inner nature?

Harvest

1 Consider what is being harvested in your dream. Is it grain, flowers, fruit or vegetables? Harvest dreams indicate abundance that is the result of your own efforts. Grain signifies nourishment. Vegetables indicate good health. Fruit represents friendship, and flowers symbolise love.
2 Harvest in dreams symbolises the accumulation of knowledge and wisdom that has been earned and gathered through life-experience.

A B C D E F G H I J K L M N O P Q R S T U V W X Y Z

★★★★★★★★★★★★★★★★★★★★★★★★★★★★★★★★★★★★★★★

Hat

1 The type of hat you see in a dream is significant of inner motivations and modes of self-expression. Wearing a hood signifies that you wish to hide something from others. A top hat means that you are being too formal in your approach. A fireman's or policeman's hat signifies a need to respect yourself, and assert your authority. A party hat reminds you to be more carefree.
2 Dreaming of a hat means that you wish to play a particular role in life. You may be in the process of 'changing hats', in a new job or relationship. Or you could be about to receive praise or recognition.

Hawk

1 Consider the factors in your dream. If the hawk is flying high, this signifies a need to take a 'bird's eye view' and increase your margin of perspective. A hawk catching prey implies that you should be wary of someone in a higher position than yourself.
2 Because the eyesight of a hawk is keen, your dream could be reminding you to look closely at a situation that you are currently not paying a great deal of attention to.

Head

1 Look for metaphors in the dream's message. You may be feeling that you cannot 'get ahead' in a project. If the head is severed, you may be feeling that you have 'lost your head' over a particular issue. If the head is uncovered, this signifies honesty. A covered head symbolises that you are not using your mental faculties fully.
2 The head symbolises the thinking, intellectual aspect of yourself. Dreaming of this can be a message to think more clearly, and to pay attention to your inner wisdom.

Healer

1 If you dream about a healer, this signifies that health worries that have been troubling you will soon be at an end.
2 Dreams of a healer can indicate that your own innate healing abilities are coming to the fore. Another interpretation is that an aspect within yourself that has caused you mental or emotional pain is now being healed, and this is leading to an increased sense of wholeness.

Hearing voices

1 Disembodied voices are common in dreams. Consider the tone of voice. Singing indicates that joyful news is on its way. Angry voices or arguing indicates that you will be disappointed or disillusioned by someone around you. Hearing your name called means that you should pay attention to an event in your waking life.
2 Dream voices are the voices of the archetypes within yourself. Listen for which ones are clamouring for your attention, and take steps to concentrate more on these aspects of yourself.

★★★★★★★★★★★★★★★★★★★★★★★★★★★★★★★★★★★★★★

Heart

1 Dreaming about a heart can signify that love is coming into your life. It can remind you to 'take heart', and to allow yourself to feel encouraged. You may need to investigate the 'heart' of a matter in order to understand it fully.
2 The heart in a dream is a reminder to access and express feelings of love and compassion. Perhaps you have been listening more to your head than your heart recently. This can also be a reminder to have 'heart', to act with integrity.

Heat

1 Feelings and temperatures within dreams can give powerful clues as to your inner feelings. Heat can be positive or negative, depending upon the circumstances in the dream. Are you 'in heat', or sensually or emotionally aroused? Or perhaps you are squaring up for a 'heated' argument, or 'feeling the heat' of being under pressure?
2 Heat in dreams can relate to the inner flame, the fire of the soul, that burns within you. Consider whether the atmosphere is comfortably warm, or scorching hot.

Heaven

1 Dreaming of Heaven does not necessarily mean that you are devoutly religious. Heaven in a dream indicates that you long for a state of Utopia, and wish for life to be an extension of your fantasies.
2 Dreams of Heaven can symbolise an inner understanding of the spiritual connection of the Essential Self that holds the threads of your conscious, subconscious and unconscious minds together.

Heel

1 If you dream of a heel, look at the context within the dream, and pay attention to any metaphors. Are you concerned that someone is a 'heel', and untrustworthy? Or perhaps you are worried about being 'down at heel', and this is a prompt to examine your finances.
2 Heel dreams can be indicative of feelings of vulnerability, as in 'Achilles' Heel'. You may be concerned that someone knows too much about you.

Hell

1 If you dream about Hell, you are struggling with feelings of guilt, fear or remorse, or you are in a 'hellish' position in your waking life. Hell dreams are high-stress and anxiety dreams. Consider whether you are alone, or in company. If others are with you, a friend may be in trouble.
2 Have you been feeling trapped or imprisoned by desires, an obsession, or temptation? Dreams of Hell can be telling you to remove yourself from an unpleasant situation before the consquences become too difficult to deal with.

A B C D E F G H I J K L M N O P Q R S T U V W X Y Z

★★★★★★★★★★★★★★★★★★★★★★★★★★★★★★★★★★★★★★

Helmet

1 A helmet in a dream signifies a need to protect your thoughts or your private space from intrusion by others. Consider the type of helmet, and whether you are wearing it, or seeing another person wearing it. If someone else wears a helmet, this indicates that they are guarding themselves from others in your circle.
2 Because a helmet covers the head, you may be suppressing your logical aspect, and not giving credence to thoughts or ideas that would benefit you.

Herbs

1 Herbs in a dream usually signify pleasure in being 'of use', and helping others. If the herbs are poisonous, this indicates that you should take care, since others may be attempting to damage your reputation.
2 Note whether the herbs in your dream are wild, or are growing in a herb garden. This can reveal whether your source of healing and nurturing is being recognised, as in cultivated herbs, or whether you need to go out and seek it externally, in the form of a healer.

Hero

1 Dreaming of a hero indicates that you are currently in need of courage or strength to face a challenging time, and your subconscious mind is encouraging and reassuring you. Because the archetypal hero is a figure who wins out against all odds, hero dreams often occur during times of crisis or transition.
2 The hero is an element of your psyche, and hero dreams can enable you to connect with this, and overcome difficulties through holding to that connection.

Hiding

1 First consider who or what you are hiding from. If this is an authority figure such as a banker, the police, or a superior at work, you are feeling overwhelmed by the pressures of your current situation. If you are hiding from a frightening apparition or monster, you are afraid to face your Shadow aspect.
2 Dreams in which you are hiding often stem from a fear of confronting something or someone with an uncomfortable truth. Question whether you are hiding from something within yourself that you are unwilling to face.

Hill

1 Dreaming of a hill means that you are facing an obstacle, or are feeling worried that you will be unable to meet a challenge. If you are moving uphill, you are struggling against difficulties. If you are moving downhill, life is about to become easier.
2 As a hill can signify a goal, consider where you are on the hill. If you are more than half-way up, you are on your way to achieving your aim. If you are at the top, success is assured.

Hog

1 The condition of the hog in your dream is important. A well-fed hog symbolises good fortune and prosperity. You need have no fears about lack. A thin or sick hog signifies 'lean' times, and concerns about your ability to have your needs provided for.
2 Hogs in a dream can reveal your hopes or fears. Is the hog 'in clover', meaning all will be well? Or is it wallowing in mud, which indicates trouble ahead?

Horse

1 Dreaming about a horse signifies increased strength, stamina and virility. If the horse is running free, this means that you can give free rein to ideas. If you are riding a horse, this indicates that it is time to 'take the reins' and assume control. Dreaming of falling from a horse signifies that you fear losing control of something important.
2 Because horses can travel at speed, dreams of horses can be a message that you are moving swiftly towards your goal. Horses can also signify that you are going to be travelling in the near future.

Hospital

1 Dreaming that you are in a hospital indicates that there is a need for healing at some level. If you are with a friend or relative, they may need your support in waking life. Hospital dreams can arise if you have been concerned about your health, but have not yet taken steps to have it checked out. Use the dream as a reminder to seek advice.
2 Consider which area of the hospital you find yourself in. If you are in a cardiac ward, this signifies a need to heal your 'heart energy', and recover from emotional hurt. If you are in a surgical ward, it is time to excise something from your life.

House

1 In dreams, a house symbolises your body and psyche. At a physical level, the rooms in the house denote areas of your body. Consider whether you feel happy or discontented in the house. If the house is familiar, this indicates that you are self-aware.
2 A house represents the different elements within your psyche. Consider which rooms you find yourself in, and observe their condition. If the house is in disrepair, this indicates that you are not taking good care of yourself. If you are decorating or renovating, you are about to experience major changes for the good in your life.

Hugging

1 Hugging in dreams represents a need for affection and attention. If you are hugging another person, this means that you need to show your affections more clearly. Being hugged is a sign that you are craving affection, and should open yourself to accepting it.
2 The hug in the dream can be interpreted as a need to acknowledge aspects of yourself that are in need of attention. Perhaps you have been ignoring your emotional side, and need to reconnect with this.

★★★★★★★★★★★★★★★★★★★★★★★★★★★★★★★★★★★★★★

Hunger

1 Hunger in dreams indicates a longing for something that you feel is missing in your life. You may be hungry for love, or hungry with ambition, or feeling a sense of loss. Consider whether you are taking steps to assuage your hunger in the dream. If you are searching for food, this means that you are willing to help yourself. If you are deliberately refusing sustenance, you are subconsciously cutting yourself off from someone or something that is important to you.
2 Hunger in dreams can signify a lack of emotional support. Use the message of this dream to give yourself a conscious emotional boost.

Hunt

1 Consider whether you are the hunter or the hunted in your dream. If you are the hunter, you are actively seeking the thrill of 'the chase' in your waking life, and need to find a new challenge that will satisfy those feelings. If you are being hunted, you are subconsciously dealing with feelings of fear and insecurity.
2 Hunt dreams can symbolise an intense search for something within yourself that appears to be elusive.

Hurricane

1 If you dream of a hurricane, this indicates that you are going through a turbulent time in your life, and are finding it hard to cope with the powerful feelings around this. If you dream that the hurricane does little damage, this signifies that matters will turn out to be less serious than you currently imagine.
2 Because hurricanes are a force of nature, hurricane dreams can be manifestations of powerful urges that you are trying to suppress.

Husband

1 For a married woman, dreams of her husband indicate that there is a close bond. The events and atmosphere of the dream determine how you interpret it. An argument with the husband can indicate tensions that need to be resolved. A loving interaction shows that the relationship will be stable.
2 If you are single, dreaming of a husband can indicate that you will meet someone who is 'husband material'. More usually, this dream symbolises the sacred marriage between the Anima and Animus.

I

Ice

1 Ice in dreams is closely connected with emotions that have been suppressed, or situations that are on hold. You may have had to put a project or plan 'on ice', while you wait for the right time. You may be feeling 'frozen inside' after a trauma, or 'frozen out' by someone around you.
2 If the ice is melting, this indicates that the situation is temporary, or that you are allowing yourself to feel again.

Ice cream

1 Dreams of ice cream can mean that you wish to return to carefree childhood pleasures. It can also reveal a readiness to accept pleasure in your life, especially if the ice cream is melting.
2 Eating or sharing ice cream in a dream can indicate that you are opening up to the idea of sensual pleasures, and wish to give more of yourself, and allow yourself to receive from others.

Icicles

1 If you see icicles in a dream, this signifies obstacles. Consider where the icicles are placed, and whether they are dagger-like, symbolising a betrayal, or melting, which means that a situation is nearing an end.
2 Icicles can indicate subconscious feelings of resentment that stem from events in your distant past.

Icing

1 Dreams of icing indicate that a treat is in store for you. They can also mean that you will be given an opportunity to display talents or gifts.
2 Icing in dreams can symbolise achievements. You may receive news that is the 'icing on the cake'. However, if you are spreading icing in a dream, this can indicate that you are glossing over a situation, and not according it the attention that is needed.

Idea

1 A flash of an idea in a dream indicates that someone or something new is about to enter your life. It can also mean that you are ready to open yourself up to some long-due changes.
2 Dreaming that you have an idea can be a powerful message from the subconscious mind. Write down what you remember of the idea when you wake, and consider it carefully, as it will be useful to your growth process.

Identity

1 If you dream that you have lost your identity, this means that you are currently grappling with changes that you are experiencing. If you dream that you assume a new identity, this can indicate that you need to make some changes in your life, and open up to new possibilities and horizons.
2 Identity issues in dreams can signal that you are in the process of discovering who you really are, and what you wish for in life.

Idle

1 If you are idle in a dream, this signifies either a need to slow down and relax more, or an awareness that you are leaving something important undone, and should spring into action.
2 Consider your feelings in the dream. If you are comfortable with the idleness, this indicates a coming respite from problems. If you feel impatient or powerless in your dream, you may be frustrated in waking life that matters are moving too slowly.

Igloo

1 Dreaming that you are inside an igloo means that you are feeling vulnerable, and wish for a retreat from the world, to the point of inaccessibility.
2 An igloo can signify that you need to step back from difficult relationships, away from the 'cold' atmosphere. Although an igloo is made of ice and packed snow, it is surprisingly warm inside. This reveals that support is at hand, even in a time when you feel 'frozen out'.

Illness

1 A dream that you are ill is an indicator to take care of your health. You may be subconsciously worried about a health matter. Dreaming that someone close to you is ill reflects concerns about their wellbeing.
2 You may be feeling vulnerable, and wish to be 'looked after' and cared for. Illness in dreams can indicate a yearning for someone else to take the reins for a while.

Immobilisation

1 Dreaming that you are immobilised or paralysed can reflect feelings of frustration and mental or emotional paralysis, and is closely connected with anxiety. You may be unable to act in a situation that feels urgent to you. Or you may be forced to wait for someone else to take action first.
2 The shift from alpha to delta waves in the brain while you sleep is marked by a physical paralysis. Your dreaming mind can perceive this, and produce a dream in which you are immobilised or paralysed.

Inadequate

1 Dreaming that you feel inadequate indicates that you are feeling frustrated about not being 'on par' in your waking life. If you dream that another person is inadequate, this signifies a need within you to assume more control of your life.
2 Inadequacy dreams can be a subconscious message that something is missing in your approach to life. This is a signal to find new ways in which to motivate yourself.

Incest

1 An incest dream does not necessarily mean that this situation could occur in waking life. Consider your feelings about, and relationship with, the family member in your dream. There may be an atmosphere of separation or distance between you.
2 Incest dreams can also be reminding you to connect more closely with that aspect of your psyche. If it is your father, for instance, you need to adopt a more authoritarian approach to life.

Inertia

1 Dreaming of inertia can mean that you are caught in a period of waiting for something or someone to come along. Consider whether you are alone or with others, and observe the details of your environment, as this can give clues as to what you are waiting for.
2 The state of inertia indicates a lack of movement and progression; a state of stasis. Look at how you can galvanise yourself in your waking life, as you may be feeling powerless or trapped in a situation.

Infant

1 Dreams of infants can mean that a happy event will soon surprise you, especially if children are laughing or playing. If the child is uncomfortable or miserable, ask yourself whether you or someone close is displaying immature, 'infantile' behaviour.
2 An infant in a dream represents your child-like aspect, and is a message that you need to make an effort to have more fun, and be more playful.

Inheritance

1 Dreaming that you have received an inheritance means that good things, including financial gain, are about to appear in your life. If you dream that someone close to you receives an inheritance, they are likely to share their good fortune with you.
2 Inheritance implies a passing on of resources from generation to generation. Dreaming of an inheritance can indicate that you are learning new skills that may have been prevalent in your forebears.

★★★★★★★★★★★★★★★★★★★★★★★★★★★★★★★★★★★★

Initiation

1 Dreaming of an initiation signifies an important test or challenge. If the initiation is your own, you will move onto a new level in your life. If you are witnessing an initiation, someone close to you is about to take on a more prominent role in your life.
2 Initiation dreams indicate that your spiritual understanding is being increased and magnified. You may be having powerful insights. Note the events and any other people in the dream, as these are significant.

Injection

1 Dreaming of an injection can be taken literally. You may be hoping for an injection of energy, resources, or money. A painful injection signifies that you may have to take a dose of unpleasant 'medicine' in the form of realisations about an aspect of yourself, in order to deal with a current situation that is disturbing you.
2 If you are injecting yourself in a dream, this means that you either have to heal a difficult situation, or find the momentum within yourself to move forward.

Insects

1 Insects in dreams, if they are distasteful to you, reveal that something or someone is bothering or 'bugging' you. Insects such as a butterfly indicate a time of transformation. A dragonfly reminds you to see through an illusory situation. An ant reminds you to focus on hard work.
2 Consider your actions and feelings in the dream. Fighting off insects indicates that you are battling with minor concerns, and missing the broader picture. Finding the insects fascinating signifies a determination to sift through every available piece of information with care.

Interview

1 There are similarities between interview dreams and examination dreams. If you are being interviewed, you may be feeling that others are assessing or judging you. If you are the interviewer, this denotes a curiosity about someone in your circle.
2 Interview dreams can arise through concerns about lack of preparation for the task you are engaged in. Consider what the interview is about, and who is asking the questions. This can reveal why you do not feel 'up to scratch' in a waking situation.

Invalid

1 Dreams in which you are an invalid are similar to 'illness' dreams. You may be fearful of being unable to cope, or you may be harbouring a longing to let go of responsibilities for a while, and be looked after or nurtured.
2 Note your feelings in the dream. If you are unhappy about being an invalid, this can mean that you are struggling with feelings of being 'invalid', or useless. This dream is a signal to take steps to be more outgoing, and to increase your confidence.

★★★

Invention

1 If you are inventing something in a dream, this means that you are dissatisfied with an aspect of your life, and wish to change it. Watching another person invent something means that a friend or relative is going through a transformation.
2 An invention symbolises the creation of something new and unusual. You may be in the process of 're-inventing' yourself, and trying out different and surprising aspects of your personality.

Invisible

1 Dreaming that you are invisible signifies that you are feeling ignored or cast aside, and that your views and feelings are not being acknowledged or taken notice of.
2 Invisibility can be a blessing as well as a drawback. If you feel positive about your invisibility, this indicates that your subconscious mind is working silently to reveal its secrets to you. Consider the motifs and elements within the dream, in order to decipher it further.

Iris

1 Dreaming of Iris flowers denotes an increase in communication between yourself and those around you. New friends may be about to come into your life.
2 The purple colours within the Iris represent spiritual insights, and the self-discipline needed in order to communicate with the deeper aspects of yourself.

Island

1 Firstly, consider the environment on the island, and how you feel about being there. A beautiful, lush island symbolises a need to get away for a while; to take a holiday. A barren island indicates that you feel cut off from those around you, and that your resources are running low.
2 You may be feeling isolated and alone. The dream is a reminder that no one is an 'island', and that you are trying to be too self-sufficient. Because an island is surrounded by water, signifying the emotions, you may have been trying to cut yourself off from your feeling nature, or attempting to 'rise above' it.

Ivy

1 If the ivy is healthy, and is growing on a tree, this symbolises coming prosperity. If the ivy is clinging to a wall, there could be problems with following a goal or project to conclusion, as someone or something is undermining you.
2 Ivy clings to its host, and is very difficult to get rid of once it has taken hold. Dreaming of ivy can signify that your persistence will pay off in the long run.

J

Jackal

1 Dreaming of a jackal indicates interference from someone whose motives cannot be trusted, and who is prepared to use you in order to advance themselves.
2 Because a jackal is a predator that feeds on the prey killed by other animals, seeing a jackal in a dream can signify that you are afraid that others may be wishing to take what is yours. This could be a genuine concern, or you could be too suspicious of others. The other factors in the dream will help you to decipher its true meaning.

Jackpot

1 If you dream that you have won a jackpot, this signifies coming good fortune. It can also symbolise money coming your way that is a gift, rather than earned income.
2 Winning a jackpot in a dream can represent a 'eureka' moment in waking life, when a situation becomes clear to you, and you can forge ahead more swiftly.

Jacuzzi

1 Dreaming that you are in a jacuzzi signifies that you need to relax more, and recapture the gift of playfulness.
2 Because water symbolises the emotions, the bubbling water in a jacuzzi indicates a happy time ahead, where you will be 'bubbling over' or 'effervescent' with joy.

Jail

1 Dreams of being in a jail indicate feelings of spiritual constriction or imprisonment. This could be through constraints imposed on you by other people, or a sign that you are holding yourself in too tightly, and not allowing yourself enough freedom of self-expression. You could be feeling 'controlled' by outside influences.
2 Jail dreams can signify that you are feeling guilty about something you have said or done, and are punishing yourself.

Jam

1 If you dream of eating jam, this can signify that something or someone in your life needs to be 'sweetened up', as the situation has become 'sticky'. It can mean that you have exchanged harsh words with someone, and now regret this.
2 Consider the other elements of the dream. You may be feeling stuck, or 'in a jam', or are searching to extricate yourself from a relationship where you feel 'jammed in' or crowded.

JANUARY

1 Dreams that take place in January can signify that you feel anxious or depressed, and are having to wait out a difficult situation before making a 'new start'.
2 You may be feeling isolated or unloved, and 'frozen out' of a group or situation in your waking life.

JAVELIN

1 If you are throwing a javelin in your dream, you are aiming high, and are determined to use your intellect in order to keep a tight focus on your goals. If you are watching someone else throw a javelin, this means that you could be envious of the ambition or motivation of someone around you.
2 A javelin flying through the air, with no visible thrower, symbolises good news coming, and possibly a change of environment. This could be a holiday abroad, or a change of residence.

JAWS

1 A dream about jaws can be an anxiety dream that stems from feeling attacked (especially verbally). Perhaps you feel that someone is deliberately attempting to damage your reputation.
2 In mythology, the portal to the Underworld, the realm of the unconscious, is often depicted as a set of fearsome jaws. Dreaming that you are entering between the jaws signifies that you are undergoing profound changes within yourself.

JEALOUSY

1 If you are the object of jealousy in your dream, this carries a similar interpretation to 'envy' dreams. It is possible that someone's motives towards you are questionable. You may be subconsciously aware that something is missing in your life if you are the person who is jealous in your dream.
2 Jealousy dreams can indicate that you are being over-protective or vigilant about letting others get close to you. Are you afraid that by giving of yourself, you will lose something vital to you?

JESTER

1 A jester in a dream indicates a need to be more 'colourful' and extrovert. Have you been holding yourself back? Jester dreams remind you to open yourself up to enjoying life by releasing pent up inhibitions.
2 Because a jester's role was to keep others entertained, and this involved wit and cleverness as well as clowning, you may need to employ all of your wiles in order to stay on top of a difficult situation. Jesters were great observers of human nature, so jester dreams may remind you that 'the joke is on you' if you do not pay attention.

A B C D E F G H I J K L M N O P Q R S T U V W X Y Z

★★★

JET

1 Dreaming of a jet carries a similar meaning to 'airplane' dreams, except that the speed of a jet is much greater. This implies a desire to race ahead at full tilt in order to reach your goals.

2 The speed of a jet in dreams can be related to thoughts. Your mind may be way ahead of your body, and you may be over-stretching yourself. Or you could be fizzing with ideas that you are keen to put into operation.

JETTY

1 If you dream of a jetty, consider where you are placed on it. A jetty signifies the emergence of new ideas and insights that are sparked by emotional upheaval. If you are standing at the edge of a jetty, you are keen to reconnect with your emotions by 'diving in'. If you are walking away from the edge, you are reluctant to face up to your true feelings.

2 You may be aware of being on the brink of new experience. Your actions in the dream will inform you as to the area of experience, and your feelings about it.

JEWELLERY

1 Dreaming of a gift of jewellery signifies wealth and good luck. If you see the person giving jewellery to you in your dream, consider who they are, and what they represent to you, as this can indicate the source of your coming good fortune. Note which part of the body the jewellery is for. A necklace indicates increased harmony in communication. A bracelet symbolises action. A ring signifies a relationship.

2 The wealth that jewellery symbolises can be internal, in the form of new knowledge or insights. Or it can represent healing that stems from within.

JEWELS

1 Jewels, like jewellery, signify good fortune. They can indicate that you value what is precious in your life, whether this means friendships or relationships, or the elements of your chosen path in life.

2 Consider the type of jewels that you see in your dream. Sapphires symbolise faithfulness. Diamonds signify endurance and longevity. Pearls represent wisdom.

JOB

1 Dreaming that you are at your place of work can indicate that you feel stressed, and pressured to achieve. It can be a message to ease up a little.

2 You may be contemplating focusing on what you consider to be 'your life's work', to the exclusion of anything else.

Jogging

1 If you dream that you are jogging, this could mean that you should consider your health more carefully. Or you may feel that you are 'jogging along', and that matters are working out satisfactorily without any need to exert yourself or go 'the extra mile'.
2 Jogging in a dream signifies forward movement, with yourself and your inner resources as the method of locomotion. Consider whether you are in company, in which case someone will help you to 'keep up your pace', or alone, which means that you crave independence.

Journey

1 A journey in a dream represents how you view your path through life. Are you alone, or with others? Consider the mode of travel. A journey by air indicates swift forward movement, and a determination to achieve specific goals. A journey by foot signifies that you wish to take 'one step at a time'.
2 Note the landscape that you move through in your journey. Rough terrain signifies that you are not expecting life to be easy. Mountains symbolise challenges to be overcome. A journey by water represents an emotional time.

Joy

1 Dreaming that you are feeling joyful indicates happiness and harmony in relationships. Consider whether there is anything in your dream that brings out the sense of joy, as this can give pointers as to the cause of the happiness you will find.
2 The natural state of the spirit is a sense of joy and wholeness. Dreaming of this feeling can indicate that you are closely in tune with your Source of being.

Judge

1 Consider whether you are the judge in your dream, or whether someone is judging you. If you are the judge, this means that you are faced with a choice in your waking life, and are trying to ascertain what the fairest decision may be. If you are being judged, you may be feeling guilty about a wrongdoing, whether this is real or imagined. Or you could be feeling 'judged' or unfairly viewed by others.
2 The judge is a manifestation of the archetypal energy of the Inner Critic. You may be pushing yourself too hard, or 'judging' yourself too harshly.

Juggling

1 Consider who is juggling in your dream. If the juggler is you, this can mean that you are trying to spread yourself too thinly, and are doing too much. Seeing someone else juggling indicates that a friend is overburdened, and needs help.
2 Note your feelings in the dream. If you are finding it hard to keep everything in the air, this means that you are stressed by pressures at work or at home. If you are relaxed and juggling easily, this means that you wish to face more challenges in your life.

★★★★★★★★★★★★★★★★★★★★★★★★★★★★★★★★★★★★★

July

1 Dreaming that it is July signifies that things will improve for you. If you have been experiencing difficulties or obstacles, life will become 'warmer' and more relaxed. A period of unhappiness or depression will soon be at an end.
2 As a time of heat, and often a holiday period, July symbolises the coming of an emotional 'summer', where you will be able to enjoy the company of those who inspire you.

Jumping

1 Consider how you are jumping in your dream. If you are jumping upwards towards something, this signifies that you will attain your goal. If you are jumping downwards (off a step or ledge, for instance), you are willing to take risks. Jumping in dreams can signify an impulsive or reckless nature.
2 Look for any metaphors. In your waking life, you may be 'jumping for joy', or 'jumping to conclusions'. Jumping dreams can be a point of reference for swift changes, depending upon the other motifs in the dream.

June

1 Dreaming that it is June signifies a warming-up process has begun, and that better times are ahead. Because June is a popular time for weddings, dreams that take place in June can mean that love is coming into your life.
2 Dreams of June can signify that a blossoming is about to take place within you. You may have been experiencing an internal 'thaw' after experiencing some sadness, and this dream reminds you to take heart, as things will improve from now on.

Jungle

1 If you dream of being in a jungle, this signifies that you are looking for adventure. It can mean that you have been feeling bored and 'tame', and feel a need to connect with a wilder aspect of yourself, and explore what is unpredictable.
2 The jungle can be symbolic of hidden aspects of yourself that are now coming to light. Because of the tremendous fertility and variety within a jungle, it can also mean that it is time to step out of your 'comfort zone', and explore uncharted terrain both internally and externally.

Junk

1 Seeing junk in your dreams can be a reminder that your life is becoming too cluttered, and that you need to pare down and rid yourself of any 'rubbish'.
2 If you are hoarding junk in your dream, this means that you are holding onto elements of the past that are no longer useful or relevant to you. Throwing away junk indicates a mental clear-out process is being experienced.

Kamikaze

1 If you are witnessing a kamikaze situation in your dream, this signifies that there is a destructive influence around that could cause harm to you and to others around you. If you are the kamikaze in the dream, then consider whether you are destructively obsessed with an ideal or a goal.
2 Because kamikaze is suicide that aims at damaging others, you may be angry and frustrated with your situation, to the point of wishing to unleash the brunt of your feelings on others who are not necessarily to blame.

Kangaroo

1 Even though they appear ungainly, kangaroos can move very swiftly. Dreaming of a kangaroo can mean that you are now in a position to pick up speed as you move forward towards your goal.
2 Observe the components within the dream, and look for metaphors. You may be 'hopping mad'. Or it could be that you are so motivated that your words and deeds can 'pack a punch' to others.

Karma

1 Dreaming about karma indicates that you feel a powerful connection with a person or a situation, and need to pursue what this means. Consider whether anyone is with you in the dream. If so, it would be helpful to explore what they signify to you.
2 A dream of karma symbolises a growing identification with the spiritual aspects of yourself. You may be feeling that things are falling into place. If you are struggling with a situation in waking life, this dream signals that matters will soon become clear, and will work out for the best.

Kestrel

1 Dreams of a kestrel are similar to 'eagle' dreams since a kestrel is also a bird of prey that can fly high and view the world from above. However, as a kestrel can be tamed and taught to fly from the human wrist, this indicates that you are ready to embrace new horizons in your life.
2 You may be connecting more deeply with your 'wild', instinctive self, and are allowing this 'free rein'. The flight of a kestrel between its human master and the skies signifies that you are allowing your mind to increase its range, and this will bring new experiences into your life.

A B C D E F G H I J K L M N O P Q R S T U V W X Y Z

★★★★★★★★★★★★★★★★★★★★★★★★★★★★★★★★★★★

Kettle

1 Dreaming of a kettle can mean that events are 'coming to the boil', or that you are 'boiling with anger' or 'letting off steam'. A cold kettle can either indicate bad timing, or a slow conclusion.

2 A kettle can signify an alchemical process taking place within you – a major change in the way you view your life – because of the transformation from water to steam. Because of its association with cauldrons, which signify a magical and nourishing change, a kettle can symbolise that you need to look for 'mind food' as well as physical nourishment.

Key

1 Keys in dreams symbolise entry to a new phase or fresh insights. They indicate that barriers or boundaries will be overcome. If you are holding keys, this means that you are ready to move on to the next stage of your life. Losing your keys can signify that a door has 'closed' for you.

2 Consider whether you have been locking away or shutting off an aspect of yourself or your life. Seeing keys in a dream can be a reminder that you hold the 'keys' to your own success or happiness.

Kicking

1 If you are kicking someone in a dream, this signifies a need to safely release feelings of anger or resentment. You may be frustrated, 'kicking out' against restrictions or constraints. If you are being kicked, you are aware of unresolved tensions or conflict with the person who is kicking you.

2 Kicking in dreams can be a message that you are inwardly 'kicking yourself', and that there are unacknowledged regrets or feelings of guilt.

Kidnap

1 Dreams of being kidnapped can occur at times when life seems to be going smoothly. This represents a fear of losing what you have, or having to leave behind those whom you feel close to.

2 You may be afraid of losing an aspect of yourself. Kidnapping can relate to changes occurring within you, in which you consciously leave an element of yourself behind.

Killing

1 Dreams of killing are a safe outlet for feelings of aggression. Consider who it is that you are killing, as they can be representative of a character trait or way of life that you wish to leave behind.

2 Killing dreams can indicate that an aspect of yourself, or an important part of your life, is being severely repressed, denied, or shut off. These dreams tend to occur during major upheaval or life-changes.

Kiln

1 Dreaming of a kiln can signify that matters are 'hotting up' for you, and that you are struggling to come to terms with this. Or you may be 'fired up', and raring to create something new in your life.

2 A kiln also symbolises a container for creativity and productivity. This can be message that you should follow through on ideas or plans that have been germinating.

Kindling

1 Consider what is occurring with the kindling in your dream. If it is catching alight, or sending off sparks, this bodes well for success and happiness. Your enthusiasm could be 'kindled' unexpectedly. If the kindling is difficult to set alight, your motivation and enthusiasm are at a low ebb.

2 Kindling that blazes strongly can signify passion, whether this is for an aspect of your life, a new project, or for a romantic partner. It can also symbolise the flame of the spirit being 'sparked up' through an inspirational source.

King

1 Dreaming of a king indicates that you are focused on holding onto or gaining a position of authority. Consider whether the king is someone you know, or whether someone is asserting their authority or 'sovereignty' over you. This dream motif can mean that you are striving to become 'king of the castle', and increase your sense of power and control.

2 A dream of a king can signify that you are accessing your 'kingly' aspect, and are feeling in control of the situation.

Kiss

1 A kiss in a dream can signify a longing for affection, and hopes of a romantic involvement. If the surroundings are bright, this shows that your feelings are about to come into the open. A dark scene around you symbolises secrecy. Look for metaphors, depending upon the circumstances in the dream. If the dream is uncomfortable, are you feeling betrayed, as in receiving 'a Judas kiss' or the 'kiss of death'?

2 Dreaming of a kiss can be a message that you need to accept and embrace an aspect of yourself.

Kitchen

1 Dreaming that you are in a kitchen can signify that something new is 'cooking' or developing in your life, or that you are 'cooking up' a plan, especially if you see yourself cooking in the dream.

2 Kitchens represent food and nourishment. Dreaming of this can be a message that you need to nourish and tend to yourself more carefully. It can also signify a need for emotional nurturing.

Kite

1 If you are flying a kite in your dream, you are aiming high. You may be aware that a gamble is involved – you could rise or fall, depending on the circumstances and 'how the wind blows' – but are prepared to take the risk in order to achieve your goal.
2 A kite that is soaring in the sky represents 'high' emotions, and feelings of joy, celebration and freedom.

Kitten

1 Dreaming of a kitten represents a need to connect with your innocent, playful aspect. You may be striving for independence, but are aware that you are still not quite ready to move forward without support.
2 Because baby animals can represent an aspect of your inner nature that is not yet fully developed, dreaming of a kitten can mean that you are not yet ready to face your sensuous 'feline' aspect.

Knee

1 In dreams, the knee symbolises emotional commitment. It can also signify humility, as in 'kneeling to pray', or humiliation if you are 'down on your knees'. Consider whether you are alone or in company, and what your feelings are in relation to any others who are present. You may be feeling inferior in your waking life.
2 Consider whether you have been 'brought to your knees' by a difficult situation. If so, the dream signals that you should ask for help.

Kneeling

1 The manner in which you are kneeling, and your feelings in the dream, provide the dream's message. Kneeling is a position that hampers movement; you are not sitting (and therefore at rest) or standing (and therefore taking action). You may be feeling that you are being prevented from moving forward, or reaching a goal.
2 Because kneeling occurs when supplicating or praying, dreaming of this can mean that it will help you if your focus is turned inwards, towards your wise inner guide, your Essential Self, or your conception of a deity.

Knife

1 Dreaming of a knife can indicate feelings of aggression and anger. If you are wielding the knife, this signifies resentment towards your victim in the dream. If you are being stabbed, this means that you have received a deep, hurtful wound from someone else. You may be feeling you have been 'stabbed in the back', or are 'deeply cut' by something that has been said.
2 Look for metaphors that fit the scenario in your dream. You may be currently 'walking on a knife edge', and courting danger. Or 'sticking the knife in', through being involved in gossip.

Knight

1 First consider who is the knight in your dream. If you are the knight, you are aiming for honour and respect, whilst being determined to remain true to yourself. If you see a knight, are you hoping for 'a knight in shining armour' to come by? Or you may be putting someone on a pedestal.
2 A knight wears armour that protects him while he engages with the outside world. You may be feeling a need to protect your ideas, ideals or dreams from mockery or misunderstanding by others.

Knitting

1 Knitting in dreams can relate to a desire to provide for others. Because of the creativity as well as concentration involved in knitting, there may be new plans afoot, or creative endeavours. This can also signify a new relationship, or the birth of a child.
2 Knitting is closely connected with weaving. The wool is knitted together to create a fabric that can be worn. You may be recreating an aspect of your life, and 'weaving' threads together. Or you may be recognising a 'pattern' in your life for the first time.

Knock

1 A knocking sound in dreams is a form of wake-up call, and signals that you should pay attention to opportunities that are being offered to you. If it is you that is knocking, you may be deliberately searching for opportunities at the moment. If you feel anticipation, this bodes well. If you feel nervous or afraid, you may feel 'knocked about' by events in your life, and should step back and get things in perspective.
2 Knocking in dreams can be your subconscious mind's way of drawing your attention to a character trait or situation that you have been oblivious to.

Knot

1 Dreaming of a knot can mean that you are 'tangled up in knots', and are struggling to free yourself from a difficult situation. It can also mean a commitment in a relationship, as in 'tying the knot', and your feelings about this in the dream will reveal how you are reacting subconsciously.
2 Untying a knot in a dream signifies that childhood issues that are affecting your relationships are about to be resolved.

Knowledge

1 If you dream that you are a repository for knowledge, this means that others will come to you with secrets, or for advice or counselling. Dreaming that you are seeking knowledge signifies that you are aware of not having all the facts regarding a situation, and should find out more before you take action.
2 Being given knowledge or information in a dream, whether through a voice or through the written word, indicates a link with your Essential Self, your wise aspect.

Laboratory

1 Because it is a place of experimentation, dreaming that you are in a laboratory means that you are accumulating more knowledge or information, and that you are looking for something new and different to your previous experience of life. This dream can mean that you are trying out a new way of conducting a relationship.
2 If tests are being conducted on you in a laboratory, this indicates that you are feeling dissatisfied with an aspect of your life or yourself, and wish to improve upon it. If you are conducting the tests, you are making changes in your life.

Labyrinth

1 A labyrinth is a mysterious place, full of twists and turns. Dreaming that you are within a labyrinth indicates confusion, and concerns about being 'lost' in your life or a particular situation. You may be feeling trapped, and are trying to find a way out or through. Consider your feelings during the dream, and whether this makes you anxious or merely curious.
2 A labyrinth can be a metaphor for the mind, and for your spiritual journey. You may be discovering new pathways or insights that can change the way you view yourself and life.

Lace

1 Dreaming that you are wearing lace signifies coming good fortune, and the achievement of aims or goals. A man who dreams of a woman wearing lace will be happy in love. A woman who dreams of lace may receive a proposal or offer of commitment in a relationship. If you dream that you are giving away or selling lace, this can mean that success will be slow in coming.
2 Lace, as a symbol of fripperies or extra decoration, can represent a need to indulge yourself more. You may have been holding back emotionally or materially.

Ladder

1 A ladder represents your aim or goal, while the rungs represent the steps you are taking, either towards or away from it. If you are climbing up a ladder in your dream, this indicates forward progress in your endeavours. This could be a promotion in your career, or a progression towards a goal. If you are descending a ladder, this symbolises a 'step' down in your position.
2 A ladder can also symbolise your path of spiritual growth. If you are ascending, you are moving forward spiritually. Descending indicates that you are delving into the subconscious in order to further understand yourself.

Lagoon

1 A feeling of calm in this dream may be deceptive. A lagoon represents emotional troubles, because it is a still pool of water, and can easily turn stagnant. You may be feeling trapped or stuck in an emotional situation.

2 You may be filled with doubts about your ability to move on if you dream of a lagoon. Consider whether anyone is with you, and any other motifs in the dream, for further clarification.

Lake

1 Dreaming of a lake indicates either a new romance, or a longing for more romance in your life. If the water is calm, this indicates that all will go smoothly. If the water is choppy, this means that there could be emotional problems ahead.

2 Dreaming that you are diving into a lake symbolises the dive into the unconscious. If the water is clear, this indicates that a situation will soon be clarified. Cloudy or murky water signifies a need to look more closely at the root causes of a situation.

Lamb

1 If you dream of a lamb, this reveals a need to connect with your gentle, more innocent aspect. Consider the atmosphere of the dream. If it is tense, you may feel out of control, like a 'lamb to the slaughter'. If it is contented and peaceful, you can trust those around you.

2 A lamb in a dream can relate to religious beliefs, such as 'the lamb of God', and signifies that you are embracing your spiritual aspect.

Lamp

1 Seeing a lamp in a dream symbolises illumination, and a time of clarity and truthfulness. If a situation has been ambiguous, dreaming of a lamp reveals that all will soon become clearer.

2 Dreaming of a lamp symbolises spiritual insights, in which it seems as if a light has been turned on in your mind. If the lamp is burning brightly, you will experience a burst of inspiration and understanding.

Language

1 If you dream that you are speaking in a foreign language that you do not understand consciously, this means that you are accessing hidden aspects of yourself that will broaden your horizons. If others are speaking to you in a language you do not understand, this signifies a feeling of loneliness and isolation in your waking life.

2 Language in a dream can mean that your subconscious or unconscious mind have an important message for you. Concentrate on the feeling of the dream in order to decipher the message.

★★★

Lap

1 A lap is a symbol of security, and of being cared for, as if you were a child again. Dreaming that you are sitting on someone's lap indicates a desire to be a child again, with less responsibility. Dreaming that you are holding someone on your lap signifies that you feel protective towards them.
2 Your subconscious mind may be telling you that an someone or something is about to change your life for the better, as in 'the lap of luxury' or 'the lap of the Gods'.

Late

1 If you dream that you are late, this signifies anxiety and worry. You may be feeling unready, or not adequately prepared for a situation that is developing. Dreaming that someone else is late indicates frustration or delays in your waking life.
2 Dreaming of being late can mean that you are pushing yourself too hard, or are under too much pressure from someone else. Consider any other motifs in the dream, and whether you feel anxious about the lateness, or relaxed about it.

Laugh

1 Dreaming of laughter indicates happy times ahead. Laughing in a dream can also be a release mechanism for tension in your waking life. If you are laughing, you are in the process of releasing some of your inhibitions. If others are laughing at you, this indicates an embarrassing or humiliating situation. Others laughing with you signifies new friendships.
2 Laughter in a dream can be a sign that you are now ready to embrace a happier and more relaxed quality of life.

Laundry

1 If you dream of dirty laundry, you may be ashamed, or have something to hide that you do not want to be made public. Clean laundry indicates a fresh approach to life, and an atmosphere of honesty. A problem that has been bothering you may 'come out in the wash' and be resolved.
2 Laundry in a dream represents the deeply personal aspects of yourself, and your private inner nature.

Lawsuit

1 Dreaming about a lawsuit can be an anxiety dream. If the lawsuit is directed at you, this means that you feel uncomfortable about a situation in which you are worried about being 'found out'. If the lawsuit is directed at someone else, this signifies suspicions that others are not acting in an open or trustworthy manner.
2 A lawsuit can be a reflection of your inner 'judge', or your conscience, that is reminding you to act honourably.

LEAF

1 The condition of the leaf, and the time of year, are relevant to your dream interpretation. An autumn leaf, or a leaf that is falling from a tree, signifies sadness that something is coming to an end. A budding leaf indicates new beginnings, and fresh hope. A mature leaf on a branch indicates that matters are coming to fruition.
2 In dreams, a tree can symbolise your life cycle, so the state of the leaf can indicate where you currently perceive yourself or your plans to be within that cycle.

LEAK

1 A water leak in a dream indicates depleted or drained emotions. You may be giving too much of yourself, either to others or to a situation that is taking up a great deal of your time and energy. Leaks in dreams are a reminder to keep something back for yourself and replenish your resources.
2 Dreaming of a leak can also signify that your privacy, or your private life, has become uncomfortably public. This signals a need to temporarily withdraw.

LEECHES

1 Dreaming of leeches signifies that you feel that the 'life blood' is being sucked out of you. Someone may be draining you of energy or enthusiasm.
2 Leeches in dreams can be connected with fears that you will fail in a situation, and that others will capitalise on this.

LEG

1 If you dream that your legs are attractive, this signifies happy times ahead. Dreaming of injury to your legs means that a setback is likely. Serious injury or amputation signifies fears that you will lose your status, prestige or 'standing' in life. Wobbly or unsteady legs signify uncertainty or doubt.
2 Because your legs are your vehicle through the world and through life, dreaming of legs symbolises how you view your ability to progress, or move on.

LETTER

1 Receiving a letter that is indecipherable signifies that you are concerned about a communication breakdown. An anonymous letter, especially if you feel uncomfortable in the dream, signifies hidden enemies, or treachery. Sharing a letter symbolises a sharing of feelings and confidences in waking life. A letter written in red ink is a warning sign.
2 If you dream about a letter, pay attention, as this could be a direct message from your subconscious mind. If you can recall the content of the letter this could reveal much about your deepest hopes and fears.

★★★★★★★★★★★★★★★★★★★★★★★★★★★★★★★★★★★★★

Library

1 In dreams of a library, consider which area of books you are looking at or for, as this can reveal which inner resources you can access to help your progress in life. Old books symbolise wisdom. New, unread books represent new experience that you are eager for. Tattered books symbolise that you feel rather 'battered' by life. Textbooks or encyclopaedias symbolise learning and factual knowledge.
2 A library can symbolise the sum of your mind's knowledge, and you can access this innate knowledge by asking a question before you go to sleep.

Light

1 Light in a dream represents illumination and understanding. Consider the source of the light in your dream. A flaring match signifies a quick solution, or a brief glimpse of insight. A flame symbolises the dawning of new understanding. A fire signifies inner warmth and illumination.
2 A bright light in a dream can symbolise spiritual illumination. It can also signify that 'light is being cast' on something that was previously obscure or hidden.

Lighthouse

1 A lighthouse is a guardian motif that warns of impending danger. Just as a real lighthouse sends out beams of light to warn shipping about dangerous waters, a dream lighthouse can be a signal to 'watch out', and be aware of a treacherous situation or person. The dream indicates, however, that you will be protected.
2 Dreaming of a lighthouse can signify that you are looking for advice or guidance in an aspect of your life.

Lightning

1 Dreaming of lightning implies a powerful force that can be destructive or illuminating, depending upon the atmosphere in the dream, and other motifs. If you are watching lightning flash in a stormy sky, this indicates insights into a difficult matter. Lightning striking an object such as tree signifies a shock to your perception.
2 Lightning can indicate a sudden flash of insight or awareness that brings upheaval, but also positive change.

Lion

1 If you dream about a friendly lion, this indicates that you are becoming attuned to your inner sense of power and authority. If a lion attacks you in a dream, this indicates feelings of vulnerability, and can mean that you are being cowed by someone in authority. Seeing yourself overpowering a lion symbolises success and victory.
2 In dreams, a lion symbolises leadership abilities, strength and courage. Lions signify that tremendous power is accessible to you if you allow yourself to tap into it.

Lizard

1 Because lizards shed their skin (and sometimes their tails as well), dreaming of a lizard indicates that you are at a transition point, and a major change is coming. This could be within yourself, or in your personal or professional life.
2 A lizard is associated with instinctual needs and drives. You may have been dealing with issues that are important to your sense of personal or professional 'survival'. Consider whether you have been 'cold-blooded' or ruthless to ensure your own well-being. Or perhaps you have remained passive in a situation that demanded action.

Lock

1 A lock can signify that something is being kept hidden away which you can access if you find 'the key' to open it. Consider any other motifs in the dream, as this will reveal the nature of whatever is locked away. If you are struggling to open a lock, you are dealing with a problem that is proving difficult to resolve. A lock that swings open indicates that the answers which you seek are about to be revealed.
2 Dreaming of a lock can mean that you are closing off an aspect of your psyche in order to protect yourself. Or you may be feeling that others are not giving you enough 'space', or are prying too much.

Longing

1 Feelings of longing in a dream indicate that you are aware that something is missing in your life. You may be focusing so hard on one element of your life that you are neglecting other aspects which are important to your inner balance and wellbeing.
2 Longing in dreams can be related to a yearning for a spiritual connection; for something that enables you to make sense of life, or the world.

Lost

1 If you dream that you are lost, this indicates feelings of doubt and uncertainty, and a 'loss' of direction on your life path. Dreaming that you have lost something or someone signifies that you are anxious, and your insecurities are coming to the fore.
2 Becoming lost can symbolise a fear of 'losing yourself' or surrendering your sense of self-empowerment or individuality. If you lose an object in your dream, consider the nature of the object, as this can symbolise losing an aspect of yourself.

Lottery

1 Dreaming of a lottery indicates that you are willing to take a chance in a situation. If you dream of winning a lottery, this signifies good fortune and possibly wealth. Dreaming that a friend has won a lottery indicates good fortune in friendships.
2 Are you taking a gamble that you hope will pay off dividends? Lottery dreams can occur when you are investing a great deal of energy in a situation, and hope that it will 'pay out' and you will be rewarded.

M

Magic

1 Consider the atmosphere in dreams about magic. If this is uncomfortable, this signifies deceit or manipulation, either by yourself or directed at you. Negative magical dreams can also be a message that what you are focusing on is illusory. In positive dreams, magic represents the use of your personal power in shaping your life, and means that you are tapping into the 'magical' aspect of yourself.
2 Dreams of magic can be a reminder to view the world and your life differently – to see the magic, the extraordinary, in everyday occurrences, and to appreciate this.

Man

1 Dreaming of an unknown man to whom you feel an attraction can indicate that a new friend or lover will come into your life. If the man is someone you know, consider which qualities he embodies to you, as this will be significant. Does he represent authority, sexual attraction, or protection? An unfriendly man can mean that you are dealing with problems with someone in authority.
2 A man in dreams is an aspect of yourself, whether you are male or female. For a woman, a man can be her Animus, her male aspect, or if he is frightening, he can be her Shadow.

Manuscript

1 Dreaming of a manuscript signifies how you feel about how you are creating or 'writing' the story of your life. Consider whether the manuscript looks old, signifying wisdom and knowledge, or new, signifying a fresh outlook or approach. A partially written manuscript means that you may need to make some life-changing decisions and should focus on what you wish to bring into your life.
2 A manuscript can also represent your state of mind, hopes and desires, or unfinished business that needs to be attended to.

Map

1 Maps in dreams signify choices about your life-path. Consider which area of the map you are focusing on in your dream. Are you keeping your attention on matters that are 'close to home', or are you looking at areas that are further afield?
2 A map can indicate that you are in the process of 'mapping out' your life, and of making decisions about what you wish to do with your life.

MARCH

1 Dreaming that it is March can indicate the beginning of something new in your life, because March signals early springtime. Consider the weather conditions, and any other motifs in the dream. A bright March day symbolises hope for the future. If it is gloomy, this can bode badly for the success of current projects.
2 March in dreams can symbolise that you need to lighten up a little, to be a 'March hare', and allow yourself to experience and express exhilaration or spring fever.

MASK

1 A mask hides who you truly are, and creates an illusion of mystique. If you are wearing a mask, this can indicate that you do not wish to reveal too much of yourself. You may be struggling with your sense of identity. If another person is wearing a mask and you are not, you may be in danger of being taken in or deceived.
2 A mask in a dream can be a message that you are hiding your true feelings, even from yourself.

MAY

1 Dreams set in May are a sign of good times to come. If you are alone, consider your surroundings. If you are in the countryside, this signifies that matters are in the process of blossoming for you.
2 May can be a metaphor in dreams. Have you been fearful or anxious, or feeling in need of help. May could mean a 'May Day' emergency call from your subconscious.

MAZE

1 A maze, like a labyrinth, is a convoluted path, full of unexpected corners and dead ends. You may been feeling trapped or confused, 'like a rat in a maze', or that life at present is a 'maze of possibilities' and you are not sure which to choose.
2 Dreaming of being in a maze can symbolise an urge to negotiate a difficult situation, and to find your way to the crux of the matter. The dream may be a message to allow your intuition or inner guidance to come to the fore.

MEDICINE

1 Dreaming that you are taking medicine can reflect subconscious health concerns, and can be a reminder to pay attention to what your body is telling you. Medicine dreams can also indicate that this is a time of inner healing. You may have to rely on external help or support for full healing to be accomplished.
2 Consider whether the medicine is bitter or pleasant to the taste. Bitter, unpleasant medicine signifies that you are dealing with disappointment, but are learning from the experience. Pleasant-tasting medicine indicates enthusiasm and a willingness to do what must be accomplished.

Merriment

1 If you dream that you are merry, this indicates that soon there will be cause for celebration, as your plans will go well for you. Being surrounded by merriment signifies warmth in friendships, and trust between you and those around you.
2 You may have been conscious of being in 'high spirits', and are determined to spread this and share what you have with others.

Merry-go-round

1 If you dream of a merry-go-round, you could be looking for more fun and laughter in your life. Perhaps you have been too serious lately, and need to break free and let your inner child out to play.
2 Dreaming that you are on a merry-go-round can mean that you feel trapped in a repetitive cycle that is difficult to break free of, especially if you are frustrated or are 'clinging on' in your dream.

Meteor

1 A meteor can indicate that you are 'wishing on a star', and hoping fervently that your dreams will come true. If you are alone, the wishes are kept to yourself. If other people are present, you are sharing a common dream with others.
2 Seeing a meteor in a dream can indicate that great changes are coming. Throughout history, meteors have been associated with transformation and portents.

Microphone

1 If you dream that you are talking or singing through a microphone, this can signify that you wish to remind others of your presence. You may be feeling ignored or not fully taken into account, and wish to gain the attention, or 'ear' of others.
2 Dreaming of a microphone can be a message from your subconscious that you are not 'listening' to an aspect of yourself that needs to be considered. It can also mean that you need to focus on being stronger or more assertive with other people.

Microscope

1 If you dream that you are looking through a microscope, this signifies a need to look carefully at aspects of your life that may appear to be insignificant, but are vital to the whole 'picture'. You may be overwhelmed by a problem or situation, but can solve it through examining the small details.
2 Dreaming that you are 'under a microscope' indicates that you feel under close scrutiny from others, and resent having your affairs 'picked over'. It can also signify a desire to find hidden meaning in a situation.

A B C D E F G H I J K L **M** N O P Q R S T U V W X Y Z

MILK

1 Dreaming that you are drinking milk signifies that you wish to be nurtured or looked after. Milk in dreams can be a sign of coming abundance. Spilt milk signifies disappointment and disillusionment. Bathing in milk symbolises a desire to return to the carefree attitudes of childhood.
2 Milk, as the first and most basic food, can signify that you need to go 'back to basics' in looking after yourself, or dealing with a situation. You may have been focusing too much on complexities and neglecting to remember the essentials.

MIRROR

1 Dreaming that you are looking at yourself in a mirror indicates a state of increasing self-awareness. Question how you felt about how you saw yourself in the dream. If you liked what you saw in the mirror, this signifies self-acceptance. If it made you uncomfortable, you need to take an objective look at why this was.
2 Mirror dreams can be a signal to reflect on an aspect of your life. If you saw a face that was not your own in the mirror, this can mean that previously unexplored aspects of yourself are emerging.

MISSING APPOINTMENT

1 Missing an appointment in a dream can have a similar interpretation to being 'late', though your view of the situation is more serious. This can indicate deep anxiety about 'missing out' on something important, or about letting someone else down who is depending on you.
2 This dream can also indicate that you are worried about not being adequately prepared for challenges that you are facing.

MIST

1 Dreaming of mist can be similar to dreams of fog, in which there is a loss of direction, or confusion about where you are heading in life. Mist, however, is lighter and more easily dispersed, which indicates that the situation is temporary.
2 Mist in dreams can signify 'mystery', and an awareness that something hidden is about to be revealed.

MISTLETOE

1 Dreams of mistletoe indicate that life is about to become happier and more stable. Kissing under mistletoe signifies a new love in your life, although this may not turn out to be a long-term relationship.
2 The ability of mistletoe to grow on host trees, to spread quickly, and to bring forth white berries, all symbolise a subconscious understanding that the physical body is fed and sustained by the Spiritual Self.

★★

Money

1 Dreams about money are common when there is anxiety over finances or resources. If you are buying articles in your dream, the nature of these will inform you as to the dream's meaning.

2 Money in dreams symbolises the currency of energy, and the details of the dream will reveal whether there is a 'free-flow' of energy in your life, or whether you are feeling depleted and 'poverty-stricken'.

Monkey

1 Dreaming of monkeys signals a need to connect more with your fun-loving, mischievous aspect, if the monkey is playful and happy. Destructive or chaotic monkeys signify a need to be more disciplined.

2 Monkey dreams can also symbolise the 'monkey mind' that leaps from thought to thought without following any of these through to a conclusion. Your subconscious may be reminding you to be more focused and less easily distracted.

Moon

1 Dreaming of the moon is a reminder to listen to the messages of your dreams and your intuition. The phase of the moon is significant. A waxing moon indicates that this is a good time to make plans. A full moon symbolises fruition and success, and a waning moon warns you to take more notice of your energy levels. Clouds across the moon signify secrets.

2 The moon symbolises the ebbing and flowing of your emotional tides. Dreaming of the moon signifies a growing understanding of the rhythms that your life follows, and reminds you to allow these to flow freely and uninterrupted.

Morning

1 If you dream that it is a sunny morning, this means the energy around your current plans is positive, and you can really 'make a start' on putting these into operation. A cloudy or dull morning can signify that you are feeling 'low' or depressed.

2 Morning, as the beginning of a new day, symbolises an opportunity to start afresh, and to put the past behind you.

Mother

1 Dreaming of your mother indicates that this is a time for nurturing and supporting. If your mother is antagonistic in the dream, this reveals fears and anxieties about your ability to be accepting or positive about your feminine side.

2 The archetypal Mother aspect represents the inner nurturing feminine that helps to hold together other elements of your psyche. The behaviour, words or actions of the mother in your dream reflect how you relate to other people, and reveal what can be improved upon or discarded.

★★★

Mountain

1 Mountains in dreams represent challenges, obstacles and goals in your life. Your approach to the mountain signifies how you are approaching challenges. If you are struggling to reach the summit, you are making 'heavy weather' of a challenge. Seeing yourself at the top of a mountain signifies success after hard work.

2 A mountain in a dream can symbolise your current perspective on life. If you are at the summit, you have a clear view, and your perspective is all-encompassing. Lower on the mountain indicates that you are only looking at part of the issue.

Mouse

1 Dreaming of a mouse signifies the ability to survive on very little, and to find new, effective ways of working with your energy. Mice can also represent the ability to observe fine details in situations. However, if you are afraid of the mouse, you may be reluctant to look at the small details or 'nitty-gritty' of a situation.

2 Because mice are small and shy, and prefer to hide rather than be observed, your dream may be telling you to be more outgoing and less retiring.

Mud

1 Dreaming of mud can mean that you feel 'stuck in the mud', and need to rid yourself of some limiting self-beliefs or conventions.

2 Mud is a combination of earth and water. Dreaming that you are immersed in mud can mean that you feel 'bogged down' emotionally, or 'immersed' in a situation. It may seem that you have mud in your eyes, and are finding it difficult to see clearly.

Murder

1 Consider who or what is being murdered. Can you see the murderer? Dreams of murder are often based on a fear of loss, and life is the greatest of losses. If the dream involves a struggle, it is important to consider what you are struggling against losing in your waking life.

2 In dreams of murder, the person being killed represents an aspect of yourself that you subconsciously wish to root out and annihilate. This can be fear, arrogance, greed, or any other quality that you wish to be rid of.

Music

1 If you hear music in a dream, this symbolises your underlying emotions. Consider what type of music this is, and what else is occurring in the dream. Soft music may be an indicator that you wish for a relaxed or romantic scenario. Up-tempo music can mean that you need to express your extrovert side more prominently.

2 Note your feelings about the music in the dream. Did you feel sad, poignant, happy or exhilarated by it? This can signify inner feelings about a situation that is tugging at your emotions.

★★★★★★★★★★★★★★★★★★★★★★★★★★★★★★★★★★★★★★★

Nail

1 If you dream that you are hammering a nail into something, this signifies that you are building on potential. Depending on other motifs in the dream, this can mean you are building a new relationship, developing work prospects, or creating a conducive environment in which to build on your current hopes and goals. Pulling out a nail indicates a desire to remove something or someone from your life.

2 Look for metaphors that correspond with the elements in your dream. Are you 'hitting a nail on the head', and having sudden insights into a situation? Or you might be 'nailing something', meaning that you have your proverbial finger on the pulse of an issue.

Naked

1 Being naked in a dream can be indicative of anxieties about feeling 'exposed' to others. You may feel that there are too many intrusions in your life, and are craving more privacy. Perhaps you feel others have been critical of you, or too curious about your personal life. Nakedness can also be linked to a need to 'bare all', or speak the truth in an uncomfortable situation.

2 Another aspect of nakedness dreams can be that you desire to be more open, and have more 'exposure'. It can signify a loosening of inhibitions if other motifs in the dream signal this.

Narcissus

1 If you see narcissus flowers in your dream, this indicates a desire to 'blossom' within yourself. Dead or dying narcissus flowers symbolise a loss of self-esteem and confidence in yourself.

2 In the myth of Narcissus and Echo, Narcissus did not realise that Echo was in love with him. Instead, he fell in love with his own reflection, and was turned into the flower. Your dream may be telling you that you are focusing too much on yourself, at the expense of others.

Narcotic

1 A narcotic drug induces euphoria and forgetfulness. Dreaming that you are under the influence of narcotics signifies that you wish to escape from problems instead of facing them.

2 Dreaming of narcotics can signify that you are becoming trapped in an illusion, and need to examine the situation more clearly, and face up to reality. Perhaps there is an aspect of yourself you need to re-evaluate in the light of day.

★★★★★★★★★★★★★★★★★★★★★★★★★★★★★★★★★★★★★★★

Narrowboat

1 As modes of travel symbolise your journey through life, a narrowboat indicates that you are moving forward more slowly than you wish, and that you are chafing at delays or restrictions that are hampering your progress.
2 Dreaming that you are steering a narrowboat can signify that your wish to be in control is restricting you from seeing or accepting other points of view, and creating a 'narrow' outlook. The dream is a message to open up more to the opinions of others.

Native

1 Dreaming that you are a native, or among native peoples, indicates a longing to enter into a simpler, more natural way of life. You may be feeling disillusioned about the 'trappings' of so-called civilisation, and wish to return to your 'roots'.
2 This dream can indicate a wish to be able to express yourself more openly, and to shake off conventions or restrictions on how you 'should' or 'should not' behave.

Navigation

1 Dreaming that you are navigating signifies that you are set on a specific 'course', and are making assessments about how to attain your aim or goal. If someone else is navigating, this indicates that you are following the lead or decisions of others.
2 Navigation in dreams can mean that you are taking steps to negotiate your way through a difficult or tricky situation. You may be feeling unclear or confused as to the direction you are taking on your life-path, and any other components in the dream can be pointers as to the best direction to move in.

Neanderthal

1 Dreams about Neanderthal peoples can be a reflection on how you view someone in your life, particularly if you consider their attitude to be short-sighted. Consider your position in the dream, and the overall atmosphere.
2 Your subconscious mind may be telling you that you need to be more 'civilised' about your reaction to a situation that is bringing out rigid attitudes, or that brings out your 'primitive' fears and anxieties.

Neck

1 Dreaming of a neck can best be interpreted through associating it with metaphors. Are you 'necking', or sexually attracted to someone? Their qualities may be reflections of elements within yourself that you are developing. You may be 'putting your neck on the block', and taking a risk. Or it can mean that you or someone else someone has 'neck', and is pushing themselves forward.
2 The neck and throat are vulnerable parts of the body. An exposed neck can indicate a wish to put your trust in yourself or another person. As the region where speech is seated, your dream could be telling you that increased communication is needed.

★★

Necklace

1 Dreaming of a necklace can signify that a romantic attachment is intensifying, and that there is a blossoming sense of commitment. A necklace can also signify honour or prestige, and praise or recognition from others.
2 As a precious object that rests around the throat, a necklace can mean that issues pertaining to communication will 'sparkle'. It can also signify messages of good news. Consider the gems in the necklace, as their association will clarify the interpretation.

Nectarine

1 Dreaming that you are eating a nectarine signifies that love will soon come into your life. Dreaming that you are offering a nectarine to another person indicates a desire for a relationship, and signals that the first move should come from you.
2 The sweet juiciness of a nectarine can represent your 'creative juices', and be a message to set these flowing.

Need

1 If you dream that you are in need, this can represent your own inner feelings of 'neediness', and highlight something currently lacking that is making you unhappy. If you dream that you are helping someone in need, this means that you are willing to give support to others, or that you are now ready to support yourself.
2 Need is connected with 'necessity', and dreaming of this means something important and vital has been knocked out of kilter within you. Consider whether your emotional 'needs' are being met, or whether you are giving too much of yourself.

Needle

1 Dreaming of a needle signifies that something is being 'sewn up' or 'stitched together', and you are bringing a situation or project to a conclusion. Look at any metaphors that are relevant. Are you searching for 'a needle in a haystack', and feeling frustrated, or is someone 'needling' and irritating you?
2 A needle can indicate that repairs are in progress. If you have been experiencing difficulties or worries, dreaming that you are stitching something together means that a resolution is at hand.

Negligee

1 The context of the negligee in your dream should be considered in your interpretation. If you are wearing a negligee, this can signify a need to relax more, or to tap into your sensual nature. Buying a negligee in a dream indicates that you are now ready to engage in a romantic and sensual relationship.
2 Dreaming of a negligee can be a subconscious message that you have been working too hard, and are being 'negligent' about ensuring that you get enough rest.

★★★

Neighbour

1 Dreams about a friendly neighbour can indicate that you need to open yourself up to a sense of community, whether this is at home or at work. A neighbour who is unfriendly in your dream can signify that someone is gossiping about you, or overstepping your psychic boundaries.
2 As each component in a dream can be viewed as an aspect of yourself, dreaming of a neighbour can be a message that aspects of yourself that you hardly notice, or take for granted, are coming to prominence.

Nest

1 Dreaming that you are in a nest symbolises a desire for comfort and security. If you are falling out of a nest, or the nest is in an unsafe position, this indicates fears of losing your security or position. Seeing eggs in a nest symbolises abundance.
2 You may be experiencing concerns about your home-life if you dream of a nest. Perhaps you wish to become more 'rooted' in domesticity, or you may be worried about upheavals in your private life.

Net

1 A net can signify entanglements. If you are 'casting a net' in your dream, you are searching for new ideas or relationships. If you are enmeshed in a net, this means that you are caught up in a web of deceit or gossip that could be harmful to your reputation, or that someone is attempting to trap you or 'catch you out'.
2 Throwing out a wide net in a dream can mean that you are opening up channels for wide-reaching communication, both within yourself and externally.

Newspaper

1 If you dream that you are reading a newspaper, this indicates a desire to gather information that will affect others as well as yourself. Consider the section of the newspaper that holds your attention in the dream, as this will reveal the area of life that your perceptions are subconsciously opening up to.
2 The area of the newspaper that you are reading can reveal any underlying fears and anxieties. Reading the 'situations vacant' section can indicate anxieties about your work. The personal column can symbolise relationship worries.

Night

1 Dreams set during the night-time can mean that something is being hidden from you, or that you wish to hide something 'under cover of darkness'. Or it can mean that a difficult period is coming to an end, as in 'the darkest moments before the dawn'.
2 Dreams of the night, especially if you have been tired or unwell recently, can be subconscious messages that you are going through a period of psychic rest and regeneration.

★★★★★★★★★★★★★★★★★★★★★★★★★★★★★★★★★★★★

Nightingale

1 Dreams of a nightingale symbolise that you will experience happiness and good fortune in the period to come.
2 A nightingale's song is astoundingly sweet and beautiful, yet the bird's plumage is plain. Dreaming of a nightingale can be a reminder to look beneath surface appearances, as hidden beauty is waiting to come to light. It can also symbolise a subtle awareness of your own inner beauty.

Noise

1 Consider the nature of the noise in your dream. Is it loud music that you can dance to, or sounds that set your teeth on edge? Are you making the noise, or someone else? Noise signifies a need to make yourself 'heard'. You may be feeling ignored, and need to 'speak up' in order to be listened to.
2 Noise in dreams can symbolise that you are concentrating too much on external matters, and ignoring 'the still, small voice' of your Wise Self.

Nose

1 If you dream of a large or long nose, this indicates curiosity, or 'sticking your nose in', and intruding on private matters. Is the nose yours, or someone else's? You may be suspicious of someone's motives.
2 Sniffing in a dream can be a message to pay attention to your senses and intuition, to 'sniff out' a deeper meaning to your situation.

November

1 November is the beginning of wintry weather, and dreaming of this time indicates that you are expecting a situation to be difficult or lengthy.
2 Dreaming that it is November indicates that a situation, relationship or association may be 'cooling' and growing 'frosty'. Consider any other motifs in the dream, as this will reveal how you can best deal with this.

Numbers

1 Numbers in dreams are rarely messages that will help you to win the lottery, but they can reveal where your focus currently lies. The numbers may be related to your birth date, or an address where you have lived. A number that you consider 'lucky' may be a message to follow through on a plan, while a number that is 'unlucky' for you may be a warning.
2 The science of numbers is viewed by mathematicians and scientists as the key to an understanding of the universe. Dreaming of ordered or tidy numbers can signify a wish to create more order in your life, whereas a jumble of numbers can signify confusion and a lack of structure.

Numbness

1 Dreaming that a part of you is numb is a message to give more attention to that area, as you are subconsciously cutting yourself off from it. Consider the area of the body that is affected. A numb foot or leg can signify that you feel unable to move forward. A numb hand can represent a fear of taking action.

2 Numbness in dreams can be related to feelings of emotional numbness after a shock or deep disappointment. This signals you to take steps to bring the 'dead' aspect of yourself back to life.

Nun

1 Seeing a nun in a dream indicates a desire for more simplicity. It can also reveal an urge to 'cloister' yourself away from the world, especially if you have been overwhelmed by activity or events. If you are a nun in your dream, you may be worried about your private life and relationships. Perhaps you are wishing for an end to a period of celibacy, or your dream is warning you about potential promiscuity.

2 Dreams of a nun can be symbolic of the emergence of your spiritual aspect. You may be focusing more on withdrawing in order to connect with your Spiritual Self.

Nurse

1 You are being reminded of a need for healing and for tender loving care if you dream of a nurse. As nurses assist doctors, you may be needing assistance with a problem that is upsetting you. An unsympathetic nurse can signify that you are reluctant to pamper yourself, and are too harsh on yourself.

2 Consider the atmosphere of the dream, and any other components within it, and look for metaphors. Are you 'nursing a grudge', and feeling angry with someone if the nurse is unfriendly? Or you may be 'nursing a project', watching it carefully and nurturing it to completion.

Oak

1 Dreaming of an oak tree indicates that there is a strong foundation in your life that will serve as a springboard to success. Because of the longevity and endurance of oak trees, the situation that you are currently involved in can be viewed as long-term. Consider the season in the dream. If the oak tree is in bud, this means that a new beginning will lead to great things.
2 The roots of the oak tree spread as far underground as its branches reach towards the sky. Your dream is telling you that you can aim high, because your ideas have firmly 'taken root'.

Oar

1 The instruments through which you guide your dream vehicle symbolise your own efforts during life's journey. Oars represent controlled movement and direction. Because of their shape they are a masculine motif, and are used to guide you through water which is associated with the emotions. This indicates a desire for control over your feelings.
2 Consider whether you are rowing hard, which signifies determination and assertiveness, or are lazily dipping the oars in the water, which signifies 'going with the flow'. Are you moving in circles, meaning loss of mental direction? Or you may be 'up the creek without a paddle' if you have only one oar, and are unable to steer.

Oasis

1 Dreaming of an oasis signifies a need to take a rest from a busy life. You may be feeling a need for emotional nourishment, especially if you have been feeling like an emotional 'desert' recently.
2 An oasis can mean that you have reached a new phase in your life, and are gathering your energy, ready to move towards a chosen challenge.

Obelisk

1 An obelisk is representative of your creative self-expression. If the stone is carved into, or painted, this shows that you are 'making your mark' on life. Consider the setting where the obelisk is placed, as this indicates your inner feelings about your ability to shape, or carve out, your life.
2 As an obelisk is a marker stone for sacred sites or spaces, this dream can mean that you are becoming more spiritually aware.

Obligations

1 Dreaming that you have an obligation to fulfil signifies that you feel bound to give more of yourself than you wish and resent this. You may be under pressure due to demands from others.
2 An obligation dream can be a message from your conscience. You may have made a promise to yourself that you now wish to forget, but your subconscious mind has a long memory and this has resurfaced.

Obstruction

1 Facing an obstruction in a dream indicates that you are attempting to deal with opposition by pushing hard against it. Your dream could be telling you to step back, and find another way through.
2 The obstruction in your dream can symbolise an aspect of yourself. Consider whether you are 'in two minds' over an issue, or are putting up unconscious resistance against a decision made in waking life.

Ocean

1 The ocean in dreams represents your emotional life, and your actions in the dream reveal how you are dealing with this. You may be sailing a calm sea, meaning that life is flowing smoothly. Stormy seas, or struggling with waves, symbolise emotional upheaval. Fishing in the ocean signifies opportunities.
2 If you are above the water, in a boat or craft, this means that you feel in control of your emotions. Diving into the ocean symbolises the urge to delve deep into your inner motives and responses.

October

1 As the time of harvest, before winter sets in, October in a dream signifies abundance that is gained through hard work and application. Developments that you have set in motion are likely to be successful.
2 October marks the life-season of early autumn. It can signify that you are now entering a new phase of life, in which your outlook becomes more mature and forward-looking.

Odd one out

1 Dreaming that you are the odd one out, and are left on the periphery, is often an anxiety dream that is sparked by concerns about not 'fitting in'. Consider whether you feel upset, uncomfortable, or content about your exclusion. Note who else is in your dream, and which qualities they represent that you may not recognise in yourself.
2 Being the odd one out can signify that you do not wish to be the same as everyone else, and desire to have your individuality recognised.

★★★★★★★★★★★★★★★★★★★★★★★★★★★★★★★★★★★★★★

Offer

1 If an offer is made to you in a dream, this means that an opportunity is about to be presented that you should consider following through. If you are making an offer in a dream, consider its nature, and who it is made to, as this reveals what you currently wish for, and what you are prepared to give of yourself in exchange.

2 A dream offer can be a bargaining tool between two aspects of your personality that need to trade off against each other.

Office

1 Dreaming of an office can simply mean that you are working too hard, and are so focused or anxious that you cannot let go even while asleep. This dream can also reflect your feelings about your sense of responsibility and order. If you are alone in the office, this indicates that you need to consider 'going it alone' professionally. If others are present, consider what they represent to you through their speech or actions.

2 A tidy office in a dream symbolises a sharpness and keenness in your attitudes towards yourself. An untidy office signifies that you are becoming caught up in rambling thought-processes that are causing inefficiency.

Officer

1 An officer in any form represents authority. If you are in trouble with an officer in your dream, this signifies a feeling of anxiety or resentment over an authority figure. If you are being helped by an officer, this indicates a need to ask for guidance in a situation.

2 An officer in a dream can represent your relationship with your inner voice of authority. This can be positive, or something that you are rebelling against, depending on the details of the dream.

Oil

1 Dreaming of oil can symbolise prosperity, especially if the oil is being drawn to the surface. Spilled oil or oil slicks can mean a financial loss. Pouring oil from a jar can signify a desire to nurture.

2 The wealth symbolised by oil can be emotional rather than material, depending on any other motifs in the dream. Dreaming of massage oils or essential oils indicates that inner healing is at work.

Old man

1 An old man in a dream can represent tradition, wisdom and mature masculinity, especially if you are engaged in conversation. An old man in tattered clothes, or who appears ill, signifies that you are neglecting to listen to your wise inner voice.

2 As an archetype, the old man is the aspect of yourself that carries authority with wisdom and compassion. He represents the Self, for a male dreamer, or the Animus for a female dreamer.

Old woman

1 An old woman in a dream symbolises wisdom and compassion, and the power of the feminine psyche. The 'crone' is the archetypal mature feminine. If the old woman is helpful or friendly, this signifies that you are paying attention to your mature female aspect. If she is ill, weak, or dishevelled, this is a message that you need to nurture that aspect within you.
2 For a woman dreamer, the old woman represents the Wise Self. For a male dreamer, the old woman represents the Anima.

Opera

1 If you dream about an opera, this indicates that a events have expanded to become 'larger than life'. Or perhaps you have been exaggerating a situation, or overreacting to it. If you are performing in an opera, you desire to make more of qualities within yourself that you wish others to recognise.
2 You may be feeling that events in your life have expanded your horizons. Or your life may appear like a 'soap opera', in which case too many events are occurring, and this brings a sense of unreality.

Orange

1 Dreaming of oranges, or orange-coloured objects, signifies an upsurge in your energy, particularly sexual energy, as oranges symbolise fertility. Orange colours within dreams indicate that you are ready to be more creative and extroverted.
2 Orange in dreams can symbolise a cheerful and independent state of mind. You are likely to be feeling increasingly confident about yourself and your endeavours.

Orchestra

1 If you dream of an orchestra, this signifies that you are now ready to become part of a group, and are willing to contribute something of yourself that leads to increased harmony with others. The discipline of an orchestra entails everyone being aware of their unique place, and not attempting to overshadow or be overshadowed.
2 The orchestra can be a symbol of the various elements within yourself that are now striving to work in harmony with each other.

Orgy

1 Dreaming of an orgy indicates a vast quantity of energy that needs to be released. As the channel for this energy is sexual in the dream, it can indicate a need for release of sexual and emotional tension in a 'safe' space, rather than in waking life. Orgy dreams can also signify pent-up inhibitions, or a fear of losing control in waking life.
2 When energy is blocked, the dreaming self may release this as intensely sexual dreams. You may be experiencing great changes in your waking life, and your subconscious mind is dealing with this through your dream.

A B C D E F G H I J K L M N O P Q R S T U V W X Y Z

★★

Orphan

1 If you are an orphan in your dream, this indicates that you are suffering from a sense of loss or abandonment in waking life. You may be afraid of being alone, or of being rejected by someone you care for. If you see an orphan in your dream, you may be deciding to nurture someone who needs your help.
2 Orphan dreams can arise through a need to lean on others for support during a difficult time.

Otter

1 If you dream of an otter, this indicates a desire to work hard and play hard. You may have been concerned that your work/life balance has become uneven, and wish to redress this.
2 An otter's dam is built in a river, and can cut off the flow of water. Your subconscious mind could be telling you that your focus has become too narrow, and that you are blocking your emotions from flowing freely.

Oven

1 Dreaming of an oven can indicate that you need to take steps to nourish your creative energy. You may be involved in a situation or plan where innovative ideas are beginning to flow. An oven indicates transformative power at work, and a time of gestation while ideas are 'cooked up'.
2 An oven can symbolise an inner transformation, in which you are casting out old characteristics that you no longer wish to display, and are developing higher qualities that you can guide your life by.

Owl

1 Owls are a symbol of wisdom, and of the ability to see a situation in its entirety. Owls are potent dream symbols that act as messengers for information from the unconscious mind. Pay attention to the behaviour of the owl, and to any other motifs in the dream.
2 An owl can be a symbol of your Wise Self, and dreaming of them can precede a spark of inner illumination that enables you to see a situation in perspective.

Ox

1 Dreaming of an ox is a message that you have tremendous inner reserves of strength that you can call upon. As an ox is a creature that has great powers of endurance, you may have been feeling that you are carrying too heavy a load, and your dream is reassuring you.
2 Your dream may be signalling you to be patient, and to be prepared to make sacrifices, as this will pay off. Because oxen are considered sacred in the East, the dream may be reminding you to acknowledge your own inner sacredness.

Painting

1 If you are painting or see a painting in a dream, consider the subject, and the atmosphere of the painting, as it may have a message for you about how you are expressing yourself. A small or complex painting is telling you to observe the details in your life. A broad canvas indicates a need to step back and get things in perspective, to see the 'bigger picture' in life. Painting a wall or furniture signifies that a 'cover-up' process is being undertaken.
2 Painting also symbolises the way you are viewing your life. Unlike a photograph which shows things realistically, a painting is subjective, and depicts a personal reality. Your dream can signify your 'inner vision' at work.

Paradise

1 Your image of paradise in a dream is borne out by feelings of great happiness. You may be wishing for perfection in your life, or for total harmony within yourself, and your dream is reflecting this.
2 The motifs in the dream that symbolise paradise for you can be a reminder to seek happiness more consciously in your waking life. Consider them carefully, as they can give clues as to where this happiness will be found.

Park

1 Dreaming that you are in a park can be message that you need to take time out to rest, relax and play more. You may be focused on serious matters that are taking up a great deal of your time.
2 A park can symbolise an ordered, structured place of beauty in which you are relaxed and able to enjoy yourself. Dreaming of a park can indicate a desire to add a sense of leisure and beauty to your life, whether through your home surroundings, or through pursuing a creative hobby that lifts your spirits.

Partner

1 If you dream of a partner, consider whether this is a romantic or work partner, and the atmosphere within your dream. You may be feeling neglected or left out, or, if the relationship in the dream is positive, you may be in for a pleasant surprise.
2 A dream partner can represent an aspect of yourself. If the figure is a stranger, this is the Anima or Animus, depending upon your gender. If you know the person, this means that you are integrating some of their qualities into yourself.

A B C D E F G H I J K L M N O P Q R S T U V W X Y Z

Party

1 Dreaming of a party is related to how you view your social skills, and how you wish to develop these. If you are usually shy, but you are an extrovert in the dream, or 'the life and soul' of the party, this indicates a need to mix more frequently with others in order to open up your life more. Dreaming that you are alone at a party signifies fears of not 'belonging' within a group of people in waking life.

2 Your dream may be a subconscious message that you are forgetting to celebrate some of the joys in your life, and should pay more attention to these.

Passport

1 A passport is your ticket to places other than your place of residence, and so this symbolises either travel, or a need to venture out of your immediate sphere of understanding, and to open up to new experiences.

2 Dreaming of a passport can occur when you are being tightly pinned down to a specific identity. You may feel that you are defined by how others perceive you, according to a role in life, and wish to be viewed differently.

Past loves

1 Dreaming of past lovers can signify a need to be analytical about relationships that have now come to an end. Consider whether you are still idolising or demonising a past lover, and step back emotionally so that you can see the relationship in perspective and move on.

2 Consider whether you are repeating, or are afraid of repeating, a past pattern within a relationship. Dreams of past lovers can remind you what does and does not work for you in a relationship, and can alert you to a repetitive pattern.

Pasture

1 A dream of a pasture indicates a time of rest and the harvesting of the rewards of past hard work. If you are planting the pasture, this means that new projects will soon move forward. If you are relaxing in a pasture, this indicates a state of abundance.

2 Consider the scenery in the pasture. Is it grass, indicating rest and renewal, or wild flowers, indicating a connection with the natural elements within yourself?

Path

1 Dreaming of a path indicates how you feel about your 'path in life', and your hopes, dreams and fears. Consider the terrain. A rocky path indicates obstacles or challenges. A smooth, straight path signifies that you are aiming for your goal. A branched path indicates choices to be made that will affect the course of your life.

2 A path also symbolises your spiritual progress, and how you are developing as you tread your 'spiritual path'.

Peacock

1 Dreaming of a peacock signifies an identification with the ego, and a wish to be viewed as attractive or as 'special'. If the peacock is friendly, you are able to cultivate yourself to fit in with those who set themselves 'above' you. If the peacock is hostile, or walks away, you are struggling to overcome egotistical or vain motives.
2 A peacock can also symbolise an unfurling of the beauty within yourself, just as a peacock's tail opens to reveal a strikingly beautiful display. This is a message to recognise your inner beauty, and make an effort to bring this to the surface for others to see.

Pearls

1 Dreaming that you are wearing pearls is a sign of abundance and success. If you dream that a pearl necklace or bracelet breaks, and the pearls are scattered, this signals feelings of sadness and regret.
2 Pearls are a symbol of wisdom, because a pearl is created through an oyster's attempts to deal with grit that lodges within it. This indicates that you are overcoming challenges, and are growing in wisdom and maturity as a result.

Penis

1 Dreaming of a penis is not necessarily a sexual dream. It represents energy, instinct, and inner power and motivation. If the penis is erect, this signifies that you are pushing ahead towards your goals. A shrunken penis indicates that your energy and drive are at a low ebb.
2 A penis also represents fertility, which can be physical or of the imagination. Your dream may be a message to connect more deeply with your creative aspect.

Photocopying

1 Dreams of photocopying can mean that you are worried about work matters. It can also signify that you feel you are repeating yourself in a life-pattern, and are becoming aware of a need to break an old mould.
2 You may be afraid of becoming too similar to other people around you if you dream of photocopying or a photocopier. There may be a struggle to maintain your sense of individuality, and your dream is reminding you of this.

Photography

1 Photographs in a dream can represent memories from the past, or experiences that you are undergoing at present. As a photograph is an image rather than the reality of a person or object, it can also signify illusions that need to be recognised. Seeing a photograph of someone you know can be a warning that there are undercurrents in your relationship.
2 A photograph can symbolise a part of yourself or your life that you need to look at in more depth. Consider the subject of the photograph, your feelings around it.

A B C D E F G H I J K L M N O P Q R S T U V W X Y Z

★★★

Physician

1 As with dreams about a doctor, dreaming of a physician indicates that a healing process is in progress. You may be feeling in need of nurturing. If you are ill in the dream, consider the nature of the dis-ease. A broken bone can indicate strained relationships, or a 'fractured' situation. A fever can signify a 'burning' question that needs to be considered.
2 Because this is an authority figure, dreaming of a physician can mean that you need to either take more responsibility for your health, or listen to advice given to you.

Piano

1 Dreaming that you are playing a piano symbolises your feelings about your creativity, and about how to bring joy into your life. Because it takes discipline to learn the piano, your dream may be telling you that you need to take responsibility and become the 'orchestrator' of your life.
2 The way in which you are playing the piano, as well as the music you are playing, is significant. If your fingers are expertly tripping over the keys, this reveals a sense of control over the creative elements in your life. If you are stumbling, or making mistakes, this indicates that you are faltering in your self-expression in waking life.

Pig

1 Dreaming of a pig is symbolic of baser traits such as greed or laziness. You may be subconsciously concerned that either you or someone you know are expressing those qualities, and are uncomfortable with this.
2 Pig dreams can also be a message that you are being too stubborn or 'pig-headed'. Consider the events of the dream, and any other motifs that are present. If the pig is friendly towards you, this can indicate a change of attitudes.

Pill

1 If you are swallowing a pill in a dream, this can mean that you are having to take a metaphorical dose of medicine. You may be having to deal with something unpleasant, but which needs to be resolved in order to regain a 'healthy' situation.
2 Consider what type of pill you are taking, and what it is for. A pill in a dream can symbolise taking action to heal a situation, or to make yourself feel better or happier.

Pilot

1 Dreaming of a pilot signifies that you are in the 'pilot's seat', and are taking control of a situation or issue that could be construed as difficult or dangerous. If you are piloting a plane, this shows that you are determined to soar above a situation.
2 Being a pilot entails the acceptance of a great deal of responsibility, and the ability to take charge of others. You may be taking on extra responsibility in your waking life, for others as well as yourself. Your emotions in the dream reflect how you feel about this.

★★

Pink

1 Pink in dreams indicates good health, and the nurturing of friendships. You may be feeling 'in the pink', or happy and celebratory.
2 Pink is the colour that symbolises unconditional love. Dreaming in this colour can indicate that you are experiencing and exhibiting this quality, and are moving forward along your spiritual path. It signifies a loving and giving attitude towards others.

Pit

1 As with an 'abyss', dreaming of a pit indicates that you are feeling overwhelmed by difficulties or obstacles. You may be experiencing feelings of depression, or are afraid that the bottom is about to drop out of your world. If you are rescuing someone from a pit, you may be supporting and caring for someone who is in a 'pit of despair'.
2 A pit, with its similarities to the Void, can indicate the death, or ending, of your current mode of thinking or way of life. Dreaming of this implies that you are already dealing with your feelings about the change at a subconscious level.

Planet

1 Dreams about a planet indicate a need for a major change, and for an increased sense of adventure in your life. You may be feeling a desire to expand beyond your current situation, and venture to discover new horizons.
2 Each of the planets corresponds to an archetypal energy, so dreaming of a planet indicates that you are connecting to the archetypal aspects of yourself. If you dream of Saturn, this symbolises the determination to overcome a restrictive situation. Jupiter signifies growth and expansion. Venus represents love and relationships.

Police

1 Dreaming of the police signifies issues around authority. If the police are helpful in your dream, you are comfortable dealing with authority, and with those who represent this. If you feel intimidated in your dream, this reveals feelings of guilt or a sense of wrong-doing, whether you or someone else is the perpetrator.
2 The police in a dream can also symbolise protection. Or you may be 'policing' yourself, to ensure that habits or negative traits do not get out of hand.

Porcupine

1 If you dream of a porcupine, this can be a message to be careful, and on your guard against 'prickly' or hostile characters. A porcupine will only attack when it is extremely provoked, and your dream may be advising you to remove yourself from an unpleasant situation.
2 The quills of a porcupine can symbolise your inner safety mechanism that warns you intuitively of difficult or dangerous situations. You may be feeling vulnerable, but this is a reminder from your subconscious that you can protect yourself if necessary.

A B C D E F G H I J K L M N O P Q R S T U V W X Y Z

★★

Precipice

1 Dreams of a precipice are similar in interpretation to dreams of an abyss or a cliff. If you are poised on the edge of a precipice, this signifies that you are afraid of failing in a situation or relationship, and are battling to remain grounded and anchored.
2 A dream of a precipice can also signal a new beginning, and a fresh phase in your life that is frightening because of its unfamiliarity. If you fell or leaped over the precipice in your dream, this indicates an acceptance of the situation.

Predator

1 Dreaming about a predator can indicate a fear that someone whom you know is taking something important from you. Or you may feel 'eaten up' by a negative feeling such as resentment, and your dream is cautioning you against this.
2 Predator dreams can also be associated with the Shadow, the dark elements within your psyche that you do not wish to acknowledge or deal with.

Pregnant

1 If you are actually pregnant, or hoping for a baby, dreams about pregnancy can be your subconscious mind's way of helping you to work through anxieties, fears and hopes. Otherwise, dreams that you are pregnant symbolise that a gestation process is taking place within you. New ideas could pave the way for something major in your life.
2 The gestation and incubation signified by pregnancy can also relate to processes that are taking place within you creatively and spiritually, and which will lead to the birth of new aspects of your Self. This dream serves as a reminder to work on developing your potential.

Priest

1 The nature and manner of the priest in your dream determines how you will interpret this. A priest can be a spiritual guide and mentor, if the atmosphere in the dream is positive, or can represent stern authority and moral judgement, if the atmosphere is negative.
2 A priest in a dream can be the voice of your wise inner Self that shines light on aspects that you need to pay attention to.

Prison

1 Dreaming that you are in prison symbolises a feeling of severe restriction and confinement in your waking life. You may be dealing with a situation that you feel there is no escape from.
2 Prison dreams can also symbolise restrictions that you are placing on yourself. Question whether you are imprisoning yourself through being too controlled or disciplined. If so, this dream is a message that it is time to reduce the restrictions and 'break free'.

★★★

Professor

1 If you dream that you are a professor, then you are ready to acknowledge the maturity and insight that you have gained through your life-experiences. If you are with a professor, this indicates that you would be wise to listen to the advice of someone whom you respect.

2 Dreams about a professor symbolise a striving towards knowledge and wisdom, and an inner respect for what you consider to be your achievements.

Prophet

1 Dreaming that you are a prophet indicates a deep-rooted self-belief, and a willingness to be guided by the far-seeing aspects of yourself. If you are with a prophet in your dream, you may be in need of help or guidance about a matter that is important to you.

2 A prophet in a dream can be the voice of your intuition, which reminds you to listen and to pay attention.

Pumpkin

1 As an autumn fruit that is associated with the bounty of the harvest, a pumpkin symbolises relaxation and abundance after the hard work of planting, caring for, and harvesting your ideas.

2 A pumpkin is carved out at Hallowe'en, and lit from within by a candle. This aspect of the pumpkin signifies that you are ready to accept the magical aspects within life, and a sense of child-like wonder.

Puppet

1 In dreams of a puppet, consider whether you are the puppet, or the puppeteer. If you are the puppet, you are feeling, or are being, manipulated to accord with the will of another person who is in control of a situation. If you are the puppeteer, your dream is telling you that, consciously or unconsciously, you are being manipulative.

2 You may be feeling a sense of helplessness in a situation that you have no control over. It may seem that you are the puppet of an uncaring Fate, or Higher Power.

Purse

1 If you dream that you have found a purse, this indicates that you are recognising something of value that has come into your life. If you lose a purse in a dream, this means that you have been neglecting something important to you. As with the saying 'you can't make a silk purse from a pig's ear', a purse dream can mean that you are refusing to be seduced by an idea or character which is not what it appears to be.

2 Because a purse contains not only money, but items that we associate with identity such as credit cards, dreaming of a purse can mean that you are dealing with issues around a shift in your sense of identity.

Quadrangle

1 Because a quadrangle is a space that is surrounded by buildings on all four sides, dreaming of this signifies that you feel closed in or hemmed in by responsibilities and the expectations of others.
2 If you are in a quadrangle, this means that you are feeling vulnerable and exposed at this time. It may seem, in your waking life, as if the eyes of others are on you, and that you cannot find a private space to be yourself in.

Quail

1 Dreaming of a quail is a message of good fortune to come. It can also indicate a longing for romance and sensuality.
2 Because a quail is a game bird, dreaming of it can be a sign that you are changing your focus towards increased self-nurturing.

Qualification

1 If you dream of gaining a qualification, this signifies a sense of achievement in an area of your life. You may have been faced with a challenge that has tested your resources, and are at the point of winning through.
2 As a qualification is an attainment that is recognised by others, and can be used to enhance your career, your dream may be a subconscious message to focus on moving ahead in your chosen area of work.

Quarrel

1 Dreaming about a quarrel can bring to light underlying tensions that you are subconsciously aware of between yourself and another person. The dream quarrel may be a pointer that reflects an attitude or actions that you inwardly disagree with, but have not voiced.
2 A dream quarrel can be indicative of inner conflict. Two aspects of yourself, identifiable by the nature of the personalities in the dream, may be at loggerheads.

Quay

1 Dreams of a quay signal a departure point in your life, where you are leaving behind your old way of life, and moving onwards. If you are looking back inland, this can signify regrets. Looking forward indicates a willingness to embrace the changes.
2 Because a quay juts out over water (as in a 'jetty' dream), this links in with internal emotions. Your feelings for someone or something may have changed, and you are preparing to move on.

Queen

1 If you are a queen in your dream, this can mean that you are hoping to be recognised as a force to be reckoned with. Are you 'queening it', and asserting yourself in your waking life?
2 A queen symbolises female authority, and dreaming that you are a queen can mean that you are ready to take on a position of leadership. This dream can reflect blossoming feelings of self-empowerment, and a sense of being in control of your life.

Quest

1 Dreaming that you are on a quest reflects an inner desire to become involved in a meaningful adventure of some kind. You may be facing challenges in your waking life that you are dealing with by identifying yourself with a hero or heroine.
2 All that has meaning and significance in your life becomes part of your spiritual quest for wholeness, and identification with the divine. Dreaming of a quest signifies that you are becoming aware of this.

Question

1 If you are asking a question in a dream, this can indicate that you are faltering, and are low in self-confidence. If you are answering a question, this is a message that you have the answers within you, and need to acknowledge your innate wisdom.
2 Asking a question before you fall asleep opens up your subconscious mind to reveal the answer you seek. Your dream may be an answer to this question, or a solution to a problem that has been worrying you.

Quicksand

1 Dreaming of quicksand indicates that you are feeling stuck, stifled, or in danger of losing control over an important issue. This dream reveals that the problem you are facing is not of your making, and that it is important to watch where you step, as the situation could be treacherous.
2 If you dream that you are sinking in quicksand, this indicates that you are feeling 'in over your head', and are deeply immersed in an emotional issue that is difficult to escape from.

Quicksilver

1 Quicksilver, also called Mercury, is a liquid metal that has unusual properties. Dreaming of quicksilver indicates that your mind is speeding ahead, and that you are reluctant to be pinned down to one specific idea or course of action. You are likely to be eluding the attempts of others to 'pin you down'.
2 Because quicksilver, when liberated from a container, separates into globules, and joins with any other globule that it meets, your dream can signify that you are longing for communication with like-minded others, or kindred spirits.

★★★★★★★★★★★★★★★★★★★★★★★★★★★★★★★★★★★★★★★

QUILT

1 A quilt signifies warmth, relaxation and sleep, and comfort. If you dream of a quilt, you are actively seeking nurturing in your life. A quilt dream can also be linked with thoughts or memories about older members of your family, as a quilt used to be considered a family heirloom.

2 Dreaming of a patchwork quilt can indicate that you wish to 'patch things up' with someone whom you have had a disagreement with. It can also signify that you are patching your life together after an upheaval.

QUITTING

1 If you are quitting in a dream, you may be feeling that there is no point in carrying on with a situation or course of action. Quitting dreams can come as a form of release during a difficult time, or can be a spur that reminds you not to give up until all avenues have been explored.

2 Your subconscious mind may be telling you to quit a habit that is destructive for you. This could be physical, as in smoking or drinking, or emotional, as in pursuing a relationship that is not healthy for you.

Rabbit

1 Because rabbits reproduce prolifically, dreaming of a rabbit signifies abundance, creativity and fertility. It can indicate success and your ability to be innovative in your efforts to attain a goal. The use of rabbits in conjuring can also indicate that you are able to 'pull a rabbit from a hat', and surprise those around you.

2 Dreaming of a rabbit, especially if it is running, can indicate that events are moving too swiftly for your emotional comfort, and that you sense a need to retreat to your 'burrow' until you feel ready to face a challenge.

Race

1 Dreaming that you are in a race indicates that you are trying to rush ahead, and wish for increased momentum in your waking life.

2 A race involves competition against others. If you are winning the race, this indicates an urge to 'get ahead'. If you are lagging behind, this can mean that you are aware of not engaging yourself fully, and that you are finding it difficult to 'keep up' with others around you. Your feelings in the dream are significant. Do you feel anxious, or exhilarated?

Raft

1 If you dream that you are on a raft, this indicates that you view your current situation as temporary rather than permanent. You may be feeling a lack of motivation or secure foundations. Consider what is taking place on the raft, your surroundings, and your feelings in the dream.

2 A raft in a dream can signify beliefs or theories that you are trying to put into practice, but which are not based on solid facts, and may not 'hold water'. This dream can point out areas where you are taking the ideas of others 'on board', rather than following your own beliefs.

Rain

1 Consider whether you are out in rain, or watching it from indoors. If you are outside, getting wet in light rain, this indicates that a cleansing process is in progress. If you are in a storm, this signifies emotional upheaval. Watching rain fall while you are indoors can indicate sadness about a relationship. Seeing others out in the rain can mean that you are excluding them from confidences.

2 Rain represents your conscious emotions. The type of rain in your dream, and the conditions around you, signifies how you are relating emotionally at this time.

Rainbow

1 Dreaming of a rainbow indicates that there is 'light at the end of the tunnel' after a difficult time. A rainbow signifies hope, and calm after an emotional storm.
2 A rainbow in dreams is a reminder that even difficult times come to an end, and that it is important to remember what is good and colourful in your life, rather than place too much emphasis on what is negative.

Ram

1 A ram is a symbol of power and intent. If you see a ram that is peaceful, or is quietly grazing, this indicates that you have support from people who are in a position to be of help. If the ram is aggressive, this indicates that you are either being verbally attacked by someone, or are in danger of being pushed into something that you do not wish to do and should be on your guard.
2 Because a ram uses its head as a weapon, and is quick to attack when provoked, you may be having to confront information or make a choice that you feel uncomfortable about. Perhaps you feel this is literally being pushed, or 'rammed', into you.

Rapids

1 If you dream that you are in rapids, this signifies that you are being carried away by your emotions. The atmosphere of the dream, and your reaction to the rapids, is significant. Are you afraid, or exhilarated?
2 Steering through rapids and managing to remain in your craft indicates that you are negotiating a very tricky time emotionally, and that you are managing to remain in control of yourself through this. Being swept away in rapids means that you are feeling overwhelmed by the force of your emotions.

Rat

1 Dreaming of rats can indicate that a situation is worsening, because of the rat's reputation for living on garbage and carrying disease. An upsetting dream about rats can indicate that you, or someone around you, are engaged in underhand or deceitful behaviour. Have you been 'ratted' on recently? Someone could be making trouble.
2 A dream in which a rat is friendly can be a message to listen to the voice of wisdom within. Rats are highly intelligent, and the dream could be a signal from your subconscious mind to use your intelligence.

Raven

1 Ravens in dreams are often viewed as a warning signal, because ravens have long been taken as a sign of coming misfortune.
2 If the raven is talking to you in the dream, or appears to have a message for you, it would be wise to pay attention, as ravens also signify wisdom or prophesy.

★★★

Reading

1 Dreaming that you are reading signifies that you are actively seeking knowledge and understanding. The type of book you are reading can help you to interpret the dream in depth, as it indicates the area of knowledge that you seek, or need to accumulate.
2 This dream can be a message to look deep into yourself and acknowledge your inner expertise and wisdom.

Red

1 Dreaming of red signifies powerful feelings such as anger, as in 'seeing red', or love and attraction, if you see a red object such as a rose. You may be stifling passionate feelings, which then emerge through your dream.
2 Red is the colour of life and death, of the vital force. Dreaming of this colour indicates intense emotions and a drive for survival, goal-meeting and achievement. Red in dreams means that you are accessing a deep layer of your inner being.

Referee

1 Consider whether you are the referee, or whether you are being refereed. If you are the referee, this indicates that you are caught between two choices, and are battling emotionally with a decision. If you and another person are with a referee, this indicates an unconscious conflict with another person that needs to be resolved.
2 A referee dream can result from internal conflict between two aspects of your personality, or two choices that you are pulled between. Observe the people involved in order to ascertain how you can negotiate between these elements of yourself.

Refrigerator

1 Because food is kept fresh in a refrigerator, your dream can be a message to look at how you are nourishing yourself. Consider the state of the refrigerator, and its contents, and think about what this signifies to you. You may be concerned that a source of inner nourishment is about to disappear or spoil, and your dream could be telling you to protect this.
2 The coolness of a refrigerator can also be associated with your emotions. Are you having a 'cooling off' period from someone that you have been close to?

Rescue

1 Rescue dreams occur when you are feeling emotionally fragile, and feel in need of support. The motifs in the dream will provide more information. Are you being 'swept off your feet' before the rescue occurs?
2 Dreaming that you are being rescued can signify that you are being tempted to lean on others, or rely on them for advice. Perhaps you are becoming too dependent on someone close to you. Rescue dreams are often a reminder that the solution to most problems ultimately lies within you, and that only you can 'rescue' yourself.

★★★★★★★★★★★★★★★★★★★★★★★★★★★★★★★★★★★★★

Restaurant

1 Dreaming that you are in a restaurant indicates that emotional nurturing and nourishment is available from others around you. The setting within the restaurant, and the company you are in, as well as the food you are eating, all give clues as to the underlying meaning of the dream.

2 If you dream that you are eating a lavish meal with friends, this indicates that you need to be more outgoing, and make use of your support network. Eating alone in a restaurant reveals that you need to open up and expand your social horizons.

Ribbons

1 Dreaming of ribbons is always a positive sign. If you dream that you are wearing ribbons, this indicates coming friendships, and possibly a lover. Seeing another person wearing ribbons indicates a lessening of cares or troubles.

2 The colour of the ribbons is significant. Red ribbons symbolise love and a joyful attitude. Green ribbons symbolise healing. Yellow ribbons signify an active mind. Orange ribbons symbolise enthusiasm. Blue ribbons signify peace of mind.

Rice

1 Rice, as a staple food, represents nourishing and prosperity. The colour of the rice is significant. Yellow rice signifies wealth. In China, red rice signifies happiness.

2 The nurturing aspect of rice can signify a need for emotional as well as physical nourishment. Your dream could be reminding you to go back to the basic elements of love and support rather than focusing on embellishments.

Ring

1 A ring symbolises wholeness, unity, and eternity because it has no beginning or end. Dreaming that you are being given a ring symbolises a longing for commitment in a relationship. Dreaming that you are giving a ring signifies a lasting attachment for the person whom the gift is for.

2 A ring has spiritual as well as emotional connotations. Your dream could denote a striving towards unity and wholeness within yourself. It can also remind you of the 'circle of life'.

River

1 Dreaming of a river symbolises the flow of your emotions. If you are drifting lazily on a river, this indicates that you feel comfortable emotionally. A flooded river signifies fears that you will be overwhelmed by your emotional tide. A choked-up or dried-out river symbolises feelings of being 'dried up' or stifled emotionally.

2 Swimming in a river signifies a desire to immerse yourself in your feelings. If you are swimming downstream, you are willing to allow your emotions to carry you along. Swimming upstream indicates a struggle against your feelings.

Road

1 A road in a dream symbolises your attitude towards life and your path through it. A straight, uncluttered, road signifies a smooth path towards your goal. A winding road indicates a need to be alert to what is just around the corner. Barriers or roadblocks signify challenges that have to be negotiated.
2 The condition of the road indicates tendencies. A clear road symbolises a determination to forge ahead towards your goal. A winding road, or one with objects in it, indicates a distracted or scattered approach.

Robin

1 Dreaming of a robin indicates that a time of emotional 'winter' is coming to an end. Your dream reminds you that spring is coming, and with that, new growth.
2 A robin is the fiercest of birds when its territory is threatened. Dreaming of a robin can mean that you are willing to fight for what is yours, and reminds you to create firm boundaries.

Rock

1 Dreaming that you are resting by a rock signifies that you are determined to retain your strength of character even when the odds appear to be against you. Dreaming that you are trying unsuccessfully to move a rock signifies that you are currently battling with an obstacle, or 'immovable object', and that it would be wise to seek a way around this rather than pit your strength against it.
2 Rock dreams can be a subconscious message to take note of the foundations that you are building in your life, as the success of your activities will depend on these.

Rocket

1 A rocket indicates super-fast movement towards goals. You may be at the brink of great success or achievement. Dreaming of a rocket signifies that events are now taking over, and you are 'speeding ahead'.
2 Dreaming of a rocket is a subconscious message to listen to your hopes and dreams, and take steps to bring these into reality, as this will change the course of your life.

Roof

1 The levels of a house symbolise the layers of your mind; the unconscious, subconscious, conscious and Superconscious. A roof signifies the cap that tops these layers, and dreaming of a roof indicates that you are 'putting a lid' on your spiritual aspects. If you dream that you are up on a roof, this reveals that you are striving to express your spiritual nature.
2 The condition of the roof is relevant. A pristine roof signifies clarity of thought, and insights. A damaged roof means that your thinking processes need to be tightened up. Patching up a roof means that you are exploring new areas of thought.

A B C D E F G H I J K L M N O P Q R S T U V W X Y Z

★★★★★★★★★★★★★★★★★★★★★★★★★★★★★★★★★★★★★★

Rope

1 Dreaming that you are bound by a rope indicates that you are feeling constrained by rules and regulations made by others, and wish to escape. You may be feeling that someone is attempting to control or curtail your efforts in waking life. Catching a rope signifies that you are hoping to be saved from a situation, or thrown a 'lifeline'.
2 A rope can also be a vehicle for climbing. Dreaming of a rope can indicate that you are in the process of rising above a situation, and that the insights that result will provide a solution.

Rose

1 A rose symbolises purity, love, unconditional giving, and beauty. Dreaming of a rose can mean that love is in the air. If you are uncomfortable about being given a rose in your dream, you may be concerned that the affection offered is not genuine. A thorny rose symbolises betrayal.
2 The multi-layered petals of a rose can symbolise the unfurling of the spiritual as well as emotional aspect of yourself.

Ruins

1 Dreaming of a ruin indicates that an aspect of your life is falling away, and that you need to build new foundations for the future. Sacred ruins can signify a connection with ancient wisdom and understanding that is coming to light.
2 Ruins can also signify an urge to tear down the past, and to destroy an aspect of the self that is unhelpful to future growth.

Running

1 First consider whether you are running away, or running towards something in your dream. Escaping dreams can signify that you wish to run away from a situation that is painful or uncomfortable, in which case it is important to understand why you are fleeing rather than facing the issue. Running towards something indicates an eagerness to speed matters up, and move forward.
2 If you are running alone, this can indicate an urge to 'get ahead' of others, and forge your independence. Running with others symbolises a need to feel part of a group. Your feelings in the dream determine your interpretation.

Sacrifice

1 Dreaming that you are being sacrificed indicates that you are relinquishing something that is important to you in order to gain the approval or sanction of others. This dream can be a message to look at what you truly want in your life, and what you are willing to give up for this.

2 Consider whether the sacrifice in the dream is made willingly or reluctantly. Your subconscious mind may be telling you that you need to let go of an element of your personality or lifestyle, for your higher good.

Sage

1 If you dream about the herb sage, this indicates that a healing process is necessary at this time. Dreaming of a sage, or wise person, signifies a need to seek advice from someone more knowledgeable in the area in which you need guidance.

2 The herb sage is used for purification as an adjunct to deep healing. This dream can be a message to purify your thought processes in order to move forward constructively.

Sailor

1 Dreaming about a sailor signifies that you are dealing with emotional baggage, and have the ability to 'sail through' the situation with ease.

2 The actions of the sailor are significant. Unfurling a sail indicates that you are ready to move 'full speed ahead'. Sailing through a storm indicates that there is trouble ahead, but you can negotiate this if you keep your mind clear.

Salt

1 Salt is vital to life, and is also a powerful purification and preserving tool. If you dream that you are scattering salt, this indicates a need to protect your boundaries. Eating salt signifies that something is leaving a 'bitter taste' in your mouth, and is repugnant to you.

2 Dreaming that you are pouring salt into water indicates you may be harbouring a degree of emotional bitterness about something in your past, and need to resolve this.

School

1 Dreams about school are strong indicators that you are undergoing a powerful learning process in your waking life. The events in the dream, and any other people present, add to your interpretation.

2 Doing well at school in your dream signifies achievement and success in your chosen area. Being unhappy at school indicates a fear of failure in your current situation.

A B C D E F G H I J K L M N O P Q R S T U V W X Y Z

★★★★★★★★★★★★★★★★★★★★★★★★★★★★★★★★★★★★★★

Scissors

1 Dreaming about scissors indicates a need to sever something or someone from your life. Blunt scissors mean that you are having difficulty making the break. Sharp scissors indicate that you are aware that a 'clean cut' is necessary.
2 Scissor dreams can also relate to a desire to 'cut something out', in order to preserve or keep it. Consider the related motifs in your dream.

Scrapbook

1 A dream involving a scrapbook is associated with memories, and a desire to hold on to the past. Consider which images from the scrapbook are holding your attention in the dream. You may be feeling nostalgic about something or someone. What does this represent to you?
2 If you are looking through a scrapbook alone in your dream, this indicates a need to remember aspects of yourself that you are no longer expressing.

Screaming

1 Screaming in a dream is often due to a disturbing dream, a nightmare, or an anxiety dream, and it can actually wake you up. Hearing others scream indicates that you have been avoiding or denying another person's distress.
2 If you are screaming, yet no sound is leaving your mouth, this means that you are feeling inwardly blocked, and are unable to 'voice' your fears or anxieties. This is a powerful signal from your subconscious that is urging you to take steps to express yourself in waking life.

Sea

1 Like 'ocean' dreams, the sea symbolises your emotions. Dreaming of a calm sea signifies that your emotional life is becoming smoother. A stormy sea indicates that you are going through a tumultuous time. Diving into the sea means that you are accessing your deep unconscious mind.
2 Dreams about the sea, especially if they feel significant, are also reminders of your innate potential, and the vastness of your inner life and your spiritual aspect.

Searching

1 Your feelings within the dream provide the key to your interpretation. If you are searching anxiously, or with feelings of distress or neediness, this means that you are subconsciously aware that something is lacking in your waking life. Searching in the context of a quest, that carries feelings of anticipation or excitement, indicates the search for the 'real' you; the Spiritual Self.
2 Consider what you are searching for in your dream. Searching for a person indicates that you are missing out on intimacy in your waking life. Searching for a place or a home means that you are seeking stable foundations to build your future on.

September

1 September marks the beginning of autumn, when summer holidays come to an end, and work resumes its usual pace. Dreaming of this time indicates that you are preparing yourself for a return to 'normality' after a period of relaxation or slowing down.

2 Dreams that include months of the year can relate to the phase of life that you are currently identifying with. Dreaming of September signifies that you are blossoming into ripe maturity, yet still retain the enthusiasm of youth.

Sex

1 Sexual dreams signify your desires, fears, and any traits that you are in the process of developing. The events within the dream, and other people with you, represent the qualities that you subconsciously feel are missing in waking life. Consider who your partner is, where you are, and whether you are alone or in public.

2 Sexual dreams are a way of revealing what it is that you seek unity with. If it is with your boss, or a colleague, or a celebrity, the dream is telling you that you seek increased authority or recognition. Sex with someone to whom you are attracted can be your mind's way of preparing you to make a move forward towards a relationship.

Shaking hands

1 Dreaming that you are shaking hands with someone indicates a willingness to cooperate with those around you. As the gesture of extending a hand denotes that no harm is meant, you may be feeling vulnerable, and need to reassure yourself.

2 Shaking hands is a sign of an agreement of partnership. Dreaming of this can mean that two aspects of yourself that have been in conflict are now reconciled.

Shaving

1 Consider whether it is you that is shaving, or another person who is shaving you. If you are being shaved, this can mean that you are being stripped down to essentials, or that you are aware that you have just had a 'near miss' or a 'close shave' with a situation that could have turned out to be a mistake or a disaster.

2 Dreams in which you are shaving your hair indicate an urge to reveal something of yourself; to remove extraneous layers and get back to basics. Shaving your face reflects an urge to further understand yourself and others, to 'show your true face'.

Sheep

1 If you dream of sheep, this indicates a fear of standing out in a crowd, since sheep are renowned for their herd instinct. You may be concerned that revealing your individuality could cause problems. Or you could be rebelling against pressures to be conventional.

2 Your dream could be a message from your subconscious mind, which reveals that you are being 'led' by a particular character trait, which is undermining other, less obviously powerful, aspects of your personality.

★★★

Shell

1 Dreaming about shells indicates that you wish to protect your emotions from the intrusions or curiosity of others. You may need a brief period of seclusion, where you can gather your strength and energy.

2 The beauty, protection and enclosed atmosphere of a shell can be related to a womb-like environment, and a desire to return to a time or place of innocence and inner peace.

Ship

1 Dreaming of a ship relates to your emotions, and an inner journey that is taking place. The conditions of the sea will provide keys to your dream, as will the people around you. A ship can also indicate a voyage of discovery.

2 If the ship is travelling at speed, this indicates an urge to move swiftly towards, or away from, an emotional situation. A ship that is damaged or listing symbolises feelings of insecurity and uncertainty that stem from emotional upheaval.

Shoes

1 Because your feet are your instrument of locomotion, shoes in a dream signify your means of moving forward, and your attitudes towards yourself and your journey through life-experiences. Scruffy shoes indicate a lack of self-respect. Inappropriate shoes such as stilettos whilst hiking indicate that you feel unprepared for a challenge to be faced. Sports shoes indicate an urge to speed matters up.

2 The state of your shoes also reflects your feelings about your current situation. Worn-out shoes can indicate that you are tired of a situation. New shoes indicate a fresh beginning. Dancing shoes symbolise eagerness and enthusiasm.

Shovel

1 Dreaming of a shovel indicates that you are mentally preparing yourself for hard work. A shiny new shovel signifies a positive attitude towards this. A rusty or broken shovel can mean that you are trying your best to deal with a situation, but feel that your emotional resources are inadequate.

2 A shovel also symbolises the urge to dig deep into the subconscious and unconscious mind, and to ascertain your true motivations, hopes or fears.

Shower

1 If you dream of being in a shower, you may be hoping to be 'showered' with gifts, or recognition. A weather shower signifies emotional release.

2 A shower symbolises a cleansing or purification process. It can indicate a blossoming state of regeneration after a difficult time. Because of the association of water with the emotions, dreaming of a shower can signify that a situation will become clear, or come to a clean resolution.

★★★

Sickness

1 Dreaming that you are sick is a sign that you feel a need to hand over your troubles to someone else, and a desire to be looked after. As well as being a warning to take more care of your health, sickness in dreams indicates that you have been taking on too much, and need to relax more.

2 Sickness dreams are anxiety dreams. Your subconscious mind may be warning you that you are ignoring or missing signs that all is not as it seems in a situation in your waking life.

Silk

1 Dreaming of silk indicates coming abundance, and the knowledge that your needs will be met. If you dream of antique silk, this indicates that you are being nurtured by memories from the past.

2 A silkworm surrounds itself in the silk threads that it spins. You may be feeling a need to 'cocoon' yourself in a comfortable, safe environment if you dream of silk.

Silver

1 Because of its use in coins, silver in dreams can represent your finances. If you dream of receiving a gift of a silver coin, this signifies a positive turn to your financial situation. If you see silver jewellery in your dream, you may be on the brink of unearthing emotional riches in a relationship.

2 Silver is the colour associated with the moon, and with intuition. Dreaming of silver can be a reminder to listen to your intuition, and follow your feelings.

Singing

1 If you are singing in a dream, this signifies a need to express yourself more harmoniously, and to access feelings of joy rather than focusing on negative aspects. Hearing singing in a dream can be an indicator that good news is on its way. The type of song being sung can symbolise your current emotional state.

2 Singing in dreams can also be interpreted as the 'song of the Self', a message from your inner 'voice'. Take care to listen to the tenor of the song.

Sister

1 Dreams involving siblings reflect an inner need for feelings of intimacy, and for being part of a 'family'. If you dream of a sister, this indicates an urge to be emotionally close to someone, and to feel cherished. If she is your sister in waking life, consider your feelings towards her in the dream. Your dream may be reflecting issues that need to be dealt with in your relationship.

2 Dreaming of an older sister represents a desire to be guided, nurtured or looked after. Dreaming of a younger sister signifies feelings of protectiveness.

★★★★★★★★★★★★★★★★★★★★★★★★★★★★★★★★★★

Skating

1 If you are skating in your dream and feel uncomfortable or unsafe, this can mean that you are 'skating on thin ice', and should avoid taking unnecessary risks. If you feel elated and in control whilst skating, this can indicate that you are negotiating a potentially difficult situation with success.

2 Accomplished skating can signify that your path through life is becoming smoother and easier. It can mean that you are honing your skills, and are forging rapidly ahead.

Skull

1 A skull in a dream can be an unnerving symbol. If you are intimidated by this in your dream, it can indicate a need to be aware of a dangerous situation. A talking skull can be a message from your subconscious mind, that reminds you to think clearly about the consequences of your actions.

2 A skull can symbolise intellectual capacity or pursuits, because of its association with the brain and the thinking processes.

Sky

1 Consider the weather in the sky in your dream. A cloudy sky signifies the loss of hopes. A stormy sky represents problems in attaining your goal, or discordance with other people in authority. A bright, sunny sky indicates hope and bright prospects.

2 The sky represents the lofty heights of the mind, and also an association with your Spiritual Self.

Smoke

1 Dreaming about smoke can be a warning sign of danger. It can also alert you to underlying tensions, as in the saying 'there's no smoke without fire'.

2 Because smoke obscures vision, your dream could be telling you to look carefully at your situation, and see what is really happening. Smoke that is thickening indicates confusion. Smoke that is clearing indicates that a confusing situation will soon become clear to you and be resolved.

Snake

1 In dreams, a snake can represent your habitual inner nature. It can also signal that you should beware of a 'slippery' character.

2 A snake carries various meanings in psychology and mythology. It can indicate wisdom, sexuality, temptation, slyness or betrayal, depending on the other factors in the dream, and your feelings within the dream. A snake can also symbolise the rising of the Kundalini, the vital spiritual force that lies coiled at the base of the spine.

★★★

Snow

1 Dreaming of a clean, snowy landscape signifies an urge for purity and simplicity in your waking life.

2 Because it is formed from frozen water, snow can indicate that you feel emotionally overwhelmed or 'snowed under', or that a relationship is cooling and this is causing you sadness. A snowstorm indicates confusion and loss of direction in your waking life.

Spaceship

1 Dreaming of a spaceship indicates a need for adventure, and the desire to travel beyond horizons that are familiar to you.

2 A spaceship can indicate a spiritual journey, and the exploration of uncharted areas of the mind.

Spear

1 A spear in a dream is a symbol of potent masculine energy, and can be a phallic symbol. It can mean that you intend to pierce through to the core of a matter, and to forge ahead, using the full force of your will.

2 If you are holding or throwing a spear in your dream, this means that you need to be more direct and assertive in your approach.

Spider

1 Dreaming of a spider can signify that you are feeling trapped, or caught in a 'web'. If you are weaving a spider's web, consider whether you are being honest and open about your motives in waking life. Watching a spider spinning can indicate positive energy in the home, and a determination to succeed.

2 A spider is also a symbol of sacred creativity, because of the beautiful and complex nature of its web.

Springtime

1 Springtime is associated with fresh growth and the birth of new life. This indicates that you feel hopeful about a new project or relationship.

2 Because the seasons in dreams signify your approach to life, springtime indicates a youthful, positive outlook, and the blossoming of potential.

Squirrel

1 Dreaming of a squirrel can indicate a more sociable time ahead, as squirrels are social creatures. Their speed of movement, and ability to climb swiftly, can also symbolise advancement in your chosen area.

2 Squirrels' ability to gather food, and set aside stores for the winter months when resources are scarce, can be a sign that you should make sure that you have adequate resources for the task in hand.

★★★

Stage

1 If you have been feeling exposed and 'on show' to other people, dreaming that you are on a stage can be an anxiety dream. Alternatively, it can indicate a desire for acknowledgement or recognition. The other factors in the dream will enable you to decipher which of these meanings is appropriate for you.

2 Life can be viewed as a stage, with each of us playing our part until the final curtain, in the form of death, falls. Your dream may be telling you to 'take centre stage', and live your life more fully. Or to 'clean up your act', and pay attention to the direction that your life is moving in.

Stairs

1 Stairs in a dream represent your steps towards a goal. If you are climbing stairs, this indicates that you are heading towards your goal. Descending stairs signifies a retreat, or a loss of status. If you are positioned part-way up stairs, this can mean that it is time to rest briefly while you take stock of resources or redefine goals. A spiral staircase can mean that you are mentally going 'round in circles'.

2 Stairs can also represent aspects of your mind. Ascending stairs indicate a heightened thinking process, and a spiritual approach. Going down stairs can mean that you are descending to unravel the mysteries of your unconscious mind.

Stars

1 Stars in a dream can symbolise hopes, dreams or wishes that may seem unattainable at present, but which you should focus on.

2 Consider whether you are being idealistic, or have 'stars in your eyes' over a situation or plan. If your dream feels exciting and positive, this indicates that you can reach your goal.

Stillborn

1 Dreaming of a stillborn child can be very distressing. It indicates that a situation that you have been putting energy into is no longer viable.

2 Dreaming of stillbirth can also relate to inner feelings. You may feel that recent events have brought out qualities or chararcteristics in you that do not reflect your true nature, and you are making attempts to 'kill' these off.

Storm

1 Dreaming of a storm indicates conflict in your waking life. If you are exhilarated by the storm, you are secretly enjoying the challenges that are being brought to bear by this pitting of wits. If you are nervous of the storm, or are sheltering, you are looking for ways in which to retreat from the conflict.

2 A storm can bring about a release of pressure and tension. You may be at 'boiling point', where an outburst is necessary in order to 'clear the air'.

Suicide

1 Committing suicide in a dream is usually associated with traumatic events in your waking life, such as the ending of a relationship, or a forced change of residence. This dream signals that you are putting an end to your past life in order to move forward.
2 Suicide in dreams can be a motif that occurs when you are 'killing off' aspects of yourself that are no longer constructive to you.

Summer

1 If you dream that it is summer, this signifies a time when all of your needs are met, and where life appears sun-filled and happy. You may need to let go of anxieties, and allow yourself to have fun.
2 Dreaming of summer indicates that you are now maturing, and that your potential is blooming. This dream reminds you that your hopes, dreams and goals are within your reach, and that you can allow the sun of your inner Self to shine through your thoughts and actions.

Sun

1 Dreaming of the sun is a sign of coming good heath, good fortune, and a blossoming in friendships and relationships.
2 The sun symbolises the awakening of your spiritual awareness. It casts light on all it shines on, and therefore signifies the creative use of your intellect. Because the sun is high in the sky and is a witness to everything on the Earth, your dream can indicate powerful insights into the nature of your purpose or existence.

Swimming

1 If you are swimming upstream, this can mean that you have been resisting the temptation to go against your better nature. Swimming in clear blue water indicates a state of emotional and mental clarity. Dark or murky water symbolises feelings of unhappiness or depression.
2 Swimming in a dream indicates that you are immersed in the exploration of your emotional life. Consider your feelings in the dream, and what is occurring. Swimming against the tide indicates an emotional struggle. Diving deep beneath the water signifies the search for understanding of the subconscious and unconscious minds.

Sword

1 A sword is a symbol of power and authority that can be used destructively, or constructively. If you are given a sword, this means that you are ready to accept your own inner sense of power, and the responsibility that goes with this. Hacking with a sword indicates a desire to rid yourself of elements of your life or of your past.
2 A sword can also be a symbol of clarity of thought, perception, and spiritual insights. It signifies the ability to cut through incisively to the heart of a matter.

★★★

Table

1 Becauses eating, socialising and meetings are often held around a table, dreaming about a table symbolises the dynamics of interrelationships. An empty table in your dream can indicate a fear of being alone, or a need to 'feed' yourself mentally or emotionally as well as physically. If there is a group of people around the table, consider where you are positioned, and what event is taking place. Being at the head of the table denotes leadership qualities.
2 The purpose of the table signifies the area in which you need to be more collaborative. A school table represents learning and study. A dining table indicates nurturing. A boardroom table symbolises cooperation in a work situation.

Talking

1 Consider who is talking in the dream, and what your attitude is. The nature of the conversation reveals inner hopes or anxieties. Talking in dreams can provide messages about communication in your waking life.
2 If you are usually quiet, and are talkative in your dream, this reminds you to be more outspoken, and to make yourself 'heard' by those around you. If you are usually voluble in waking life, but quiet in your dream, this reminds you to listen to others more. This dream can be a reminder to listen to your inner voice, which is often drowned out by the humdrum of daily life.

Tattoo

1 Dreaming of a tattoo signifies that something in your waking life has made a deep and indelible impression that you wish, or need, to remember. A tattoo is a permanent reminder of a specific stage or experience in your life.
2 Consider the image of the tattoo, and what this represents to you personally. This is often related to a memory that you need to bring back to the conscious mind in order to deal with an experience that has 'marked' you.

Teacher

1 A teacher in a dream signifies a search for understanding and knowledge. Consider what the teacher is saying or doing, as this points towards something that you currently need to learn. Your attitude towards the teacher is relevant. Are you taking in the lesson with eagerness or enthusiasm? Or are you reluctant to learn the lesson?
2 If you are the teacher in your dream, this indicates a desire to access your own inner knowledge. Think carefully about what your dream self has to say to you.

★★★

Teeth

1 Dreams about your teeth indicate that you are at the end of a phase of your life, and are beginning a new stage. If you are pulling out your teeth, you are nervous about a situation that you are becoming involved in. Admiring your teeth indicates hope for a positive outcome, and confidence in your ability to win through.
2 Teeth falling out, as well as warning you about possible health concerns, can also indicate your hopes and fears. You may feel that a situation is as traumatic as 'pulling teeth'. Are you losing your 'bite', or the ability to defend yourself? Or you could be worrying about a decline in self-image.

Telephone

1 Dreaming that you are talking on the telephone indicates that you are reluctant to deal with a situation 'face to face', and need to maintain some distance. You may be seeking to avoid or bypass an issue.
2 A telephone motif in your dream can be a conduit for communication with the deep aspects of yourself. Listen to what is said, and how it is said, as this can reveal the voice of inner promptings.

Tent

1 A tent is a temporary and basic shelter from the elements. You may be feeling a need to 'get away from it all', and to take a break from responsibilities, and observe a more simple, natural way of life.
2 Dreaming of a tent also indicates a feeling of impermanence. You may be feeling the need to move on, and to avoid putting down roots or building a solid foundation in your current situation.

Thaw

1 Because of its connection with water, dreams involving a thaw represent the emotions. This indicates that a difficult or frustrating time, in which you have felt blocked or frozen, is coming to an end.
2 You may have been holding yourself back emotionally, or perhaps you have been afraid to make a commitment. Dreaming of a thaw signifies that you are now ready and able to move forward.

Thief

1 If you dream that a thief is taking something from you, this indicates underhand dealings that you need to become aware of. If you are the thief in your dream, there is a need to examine whether you are being totally honest about something in waking life.
2 Dreaming of a thief does not necessarily mean that something will be taken from you. Thieves in dreams can also relate to energy, emotion, or current projects. Consider whether someone is preying on your emotions, or stealing your ideas.

A B C D E F G H I J K L M N O P Q R S T U V W X Y Z

★★★

THIRST

1 Dreaming that you are thirsty indicates that where emotional nourishment or nurturing are concerned, your needs are not being met. Helping to relieve another person's thirst indicates a kind and giving emotional nature.
2 Consider what you may be 'thirsting' for. This dream can be a message to follow your hopes, or your visions, and to pay attention to what inspires you.

THROAT

1 The throat in dreams represents the vulnerable aspects of yourself. An animal wishing to show submission will reveal its throat to the attacker. You may be feeling overwhelmed or overpowered in waking life.
2 Dreaming of a throat can also represent communication, and a need to listen to your inner voice. A sore or injured throat means that you are concerned about speaking out, or afraid to defend yourself.

THUNDER

1 Dreaming of thunder signifies that emotional disturbances are brewing just beneath the surface. This can be a warning to be aware of how you are reacting to a situation that you find disturbing.
2 You may be on the verge of an emotional outburst. Thunder can be destructive, but if rain (in the form of tears) follows, it can also be cleansing. If you are bottling up your feelings, look at how you can release these safely.

TICKLING

1 Tickling in dreams signifies a need to recapture the playful, innocent approach of childhood. Perhaps you have been taking life too seriously, and need to 'lighten up'.
2 Tickling can be a release, and also a way of moving close to someone in a playful situation. You may be wishing to deepen a friendship into a relationship. If so, try a 'light' approach.

TIGER

1 Dreaming of a tiger symbolises your relationship with your inner power, sensuality, tenacity and courage. If the tiger is friendly, you are comfortable with your sense of empowerment. Being attacked by a tiger indicates that you have concerns that your power is being taken from you.
2 A tiger can provide clues as to your feelings about a relationship. If the tiger is domineering or intimidating, this indicates issues over control in a relationship. A 'pussy cat' tiger symbolises warmth and companionship.

★★★

Toilet

1 A toilet in dreams signifies emotions that are being held in check, and which you find awkward or embarrassing. Toilets symbolise that which you wish to remain private. A blocked toilet indicates blocked emotions.
2 Dreaming about a toilet can signify a need to 'let go' or release repressive attitudes or feelings. Flushing a toilet indicates that inwardly you have moved away from a situation, and are now freed up emotionally.

Tornado

1 The speed and power of a tornado in dreams symbolises a whirlwind of emotions that, if unleashed carelessly, could be destructive to yourself as well as others.
2 You may be feeling caught up in events or a situation that appear to be beyond your control. A tornado can also symbolise distress and confusion due to having too much to cope with.

Torrent

1 Dreaming of a torrent can mean that you are feeling overwhelmed and in danger of 'going under' due to too much pressure. This dream warns you to find a way to slow down, and look for ways in which to make your load less of a burden.
2 A torrent symbolises turbulent, overwhelming emotions. You may be feeling shaken up or disturbed about a situation.

Tower

1 The type of tower is significant. A look-out tower warns you to be aware of what is happening around you, and to be on your guard if necessary. A prison tower symbolises feelings of being trapped, or of being removed from something that is important to you. An 'ivory tower' that is beautiful but inaccessible indicates that you are closing yourself off, or separating yourself from the reality of a situation.
2 Buildings in a dream represent the Self, and how you view yourself in relationship to people around you. The scenario within the dream indicates how you would interpret this. You may be feeling trapped and in need of rescue, or wish to rescue someone else. If you are surveying the landscape from a tower, this signifies increased self-confidence.

Toy

1 Dreaming about toys indicates a need to explore the childlike, playful elements within yourself. You may be taking life too seriously, and need to relax and have more fun.
2 Are you currently 'toying' with a new idea? Toys can provide an outlet for the imagination, so your dream may be signalling a need to explore the adventurous, imaginative aspects of yourself.

★★★

Train

1 Dreaming of a train represents how you view your journey through life. Because of the linked carriages within a train, this also connects your life journey to that of others around you. If the train is late, you may be concerned that you are missing opportunities. A fast train symbolises a speeding up of events.
2 The circumstances on the train reveal your inner thoughts about your life situation. If you cannot find your luggage, this indicates that you do not feel prepared for what you are setting out to accomplish. Because trains have a set destination, your feelings in the dream reveal how you truly feel about where you are heading.

Trap

1 Dreams in which you are trapped relate directly to your feelings about circumstances that you are dealing with. This indicates that you are feeling unable to move away from, or escape from, something that you do not wish to be involved in.
2 If you escape from a trap in your dream, this reveals that you are now prepared to leave the past behind, and move on.

Treasure

1 If you dream about treasure, this indicates that you are discovering what is of value in your life. A treasure hunt involves a process of searching and discovery, so your dream may be telling you to map out the course that is most likely to lead you to your goal.
2 Treasure in dreams also signifies the hidden treasure within yourself, in the form of gifts, talents and abilities that can be developed.

Tree

1 Dreaming of a tree signifies a growing awareness that your 'roots' provide the foundation that you grow through and from. This dream is a message to create a firm base from which you can blossom and grow. A tree in bud indicates new beginnings. A tree bearing fruit symbolises that plans or projects are coming to fruition.
2 A tree also represents the unified aspects of yourself. The roots are your base, or foundation. The trunk is your growth process or attitudes towards life. The branches represent the different aspects of your life.

Trial

1 If you dream that you are on trial, this means that you are feeling observed and judged by others. Consider whether you are defensive, or rebellious in this dream, as this can reveal how you are inwardly feeling about the situation.
2 As each element within a dream can be interpreted as an aspect of yourself, you can view the different characters of the person on trial, the judge, and the jury, as being aspects of you. Are you feeling guilty about something? You may be judging yourself over an attitude or situation.

Trophy

1 A trophy signifies achievement and recognition. If you are being given a trophy in your dream, this indicates that you are being acknowledged for your contributions or accomplishments. Having a trophy taken from you signifies that you feel unrewarded for your efforts in waking life.
2 Your subconscious mind may be reminding you to focus on your achievements. You may be letting this slip, or taking them too lightly.

Turkey

1 Dreaming of a turkey signifies abundance and goodwill. As a turkey is often cooked at celebrations such as Christmas, you may be feeling a need to congratulate yourself.
2 A 'turkey' is also a metaphor for something that is not 'working' effectively. If the dream feels uncomfortable, consider whether you may be doubtful about the efficiency of a plan or project. Your dream may be telling you to tighten up your thinking around this.

Tunnel

1 A tunnel in dreams can be viewed as a birth canal. This signifies the transition from one state of being to another, and indicates forward movement into a new phase of life.
2 A tunnel denotes the exploration of the subconscious and conscious mind. If you see 'light at the end of the tunnel', this means that a difficult time is coming to an end, and a new beginning is imminent. A blocked tunnel indicates obstacles that need to be negotiated before a situation can be resolved.

Turtle

1 Dreaming of a turtle can indicate that you feel that matters are moving too slowly. Your dream is telling you to persevere. Alternatively, because a turtle is vulnerable and defenceless without its shell, you may be feeling emotionally exposed and fragile, and are looking for ways in which to feel safe or protected.
2 Because turtles live in water but lay their eggs on land, this symbolises the connection between your emotions and your conscious, waking mind.

Twins

1 If you dream of twins, this is reminding you that there are two aspects to a situation. You may be focusing on one, and excluding the other. Twins can also represent closeness, security and intimacy.
2 Twins in a dream also symbolise the dual aspect of your nature: the light and the shadow. The actions within the dream will enable you to understand which of these are prevalent at this time. If the twins are caring towards each other, this indicates that you are working in harmony with yourself. A conflict between the twins indicates inner conflict that you should work to resolve.

UFO

1 Dreaming of a UFO indicates that you are negotiating unfamiliar territory. The area that you are dealing with may seem uncomfortable, frightening, or exciting, depending on your feelings in the dream, and is taking you beyond your usual sphere of experience.
2 You may be feeling set apart or alienated from others, and are trying to find a place for yourself. UFO dreams often mean that you feel like a 'square peg in a round hole'. If you connect with aliens in your dream, this signifies a need to find a way in which to 'belong'.

Ugliness

1 Dreaming about ugliness signifies a state of unhappiness and cynicism. You may be dealing with an 'ugly' situation, or a hostile person. Your actions in the dream will provide clues as to how you can resolve this.
2 Ugliness manifests in dreams when you are facing aspects of yourself that you are rejecting, because they do not conform to your view of yourself. This dream can be a message to confront your Shadow, and acknowledge this.

Ulcer

1 Someone may be a 'thorn in your side' if you dream of an ulcer. Consider any situations that need healing.
2 Is something 'eating at you'? An ulcer is caused by corrosive acids, so you may be 'swallowing' feelings of bitterness or resentment.

Ultimatum

1 Dreaming about an ultimatum indicates that a situation has reached its peak. If you are giving the ultimatum, you have reached a point of feeling forced to act decisively. If you are receiving an ultimatum, this indicates that it is time to stop procrastinating.
2 An ultimatum in dreams can be your subconscious mind's way of telling you that it is time to resolve a conflict between aspects of yourself.

Umbilical cord

1 If you dream of an umbilical cord, consider whom you are attached to in your dream. The umbilical cord symbolises a state of dependency, and a need to be nourished by another person. You may be feeling weak or vulnerable.
2 The umbilical cord is a transmitter of life-energy. Consider what you can access within yourself that will enable you to feel supported and nourished. A silver cord in a dream represents the connection between the physical body and the astral body, which drifts away while you sleep.

★★★

Umbrella

1 An umbrella signifies protection from the elements. Dreaming that you are holding an umbrella indicates that you feel a need to shelter from painful emotions, or distance yourself from an upsetting situation.
2 Your subconscious mind is reminding you that you have access to your inner resources of protection and security. Your dream is a message to tap into your inner strength.

Unarmed

1 If you are under attack in a dream, and are unarmed and unable to defend yourself, this indicates that you are feeling fragile and vulnerable in a situation in your waking life. The components of the dream can provide clues as to how to deal with this, and show whether it is best to disarm your opponent, or to retreat.
2 Being unarmed in a dream is a metaphor for not being able to use your 'arms' and to take action. You may be hesitating over a decision that needs to be made.

Uncle

1 Dreaming of an uncle can mean that you are dealing with a situation in which your desire to move closer is being held back by opposition. Because an uncle is a step removed from your immediate family, this can indicate that the emotional closeness that you hope for is not as imminent as you would wish it to be.
2 Your subconscious mind may be sending you a message to allow yourself to confide in someone whom you can trust. An uncle in dreams represents a family member who is detached enough to provide advice, without being caught up in emotional dynamics.

Uncouth

1 If you are being uncouth in a dream, this indicates suppressed anger or resentment. If another person is being uncouth, you may be seeing qualities in someone that you would prefer to ignore, and are having to confront the whole picture, rather than what you wish to see.
2 Uncouthness is a form of rebellion against the status quo. Your subconscious mind is telling you that you are inwardly feeling stifled by either your own expectations of yourself, or the expectations of others close to you, and it is time to make a stand for what you believe in.

Uncover

1 Consider what you are uncovering in your dream. If this is treasure, hidden gifts or talents are surfacing. If you are uncovering something unpleasant, this indicates a suspicion about someone or something in waking life.
2 The object or person that you are uncovering in your dream is an aspect of yourself that you have either buried or been unaware of. Your subconscious mind is telling you to bring this into the light of the conscious mind, for examination and integration.

Underground

1 Dreaming that you are underground signifies that you are connecting with the depths of your subconscious mind. The events in the dream, and your feelings about those, reveal the nature of what is being disclosed to you.

2 The scene in your dream is revealing. If you are in an underground train, this signifies a journey that enables you to understand and come to terms with deep fears or desires. A cavern represents hidden knowledge that is about to come to light.

Undernourished

1 If you are undernourished in your dream, this is a warning to take care of yourself, and to focus on what will nurture you. If you see an undernourished person or creature in your dreams, consider what this represents to you, as it indicates a need to nurture that element of yourself.

2 Your subconscious mind is telling you that you are ignoring an important element within your psyche, and that if you ignore this, it will shrivel away. Consider what is missing in your life, and whether you are focusing on your intellect and setting aside your emotions.

Undertaking

1 An undertaking in a dream is similar to a quest. It indicates that you are searching for something that will expand your mental, emotional and spiritual horizons.

2 You may have made a promise to yourself that involves a more intense focus on a goal or a dream, and your subconscious mind is reminding you of this.

Underwear

1 Dreaming that you are in your underwear can indicate a fear that something which you wish to keep hidden is coming to light. Underwear dreams often arise from feelings of vulnerability, especially if you are in a state of undress, and other people are clothed. You may be feeling raw or exposed emotionally.

2 Underwear dreams can be a message that something deeply buried in the subconscious mind is being brought to the surface, and needs to be examined.

Undress

1 In dreams, clothes symbolise how we appear to those around us. Undressing in a dream signifies that you wish to 'strip' yourself of extraneous issues, and desire a state of openness and honesty.

2 Undressing in dreams indicates a need to be viewed as you truly are, with no pretence. This dream reveals that you wish to be viewed as authentic, as being true to yourself. The dream can also be a message to explore and to uncover your inner feelings and motivations.

★★

Unemployment

1 Dreaming that you are unemployed can be due to fears of failure coming to the surface. Consider whether you are concerned about your work in your waking life.
2 A dream about unemployment can be a subconscious message that you are not making good use of your potential. Consider what you can develop that has been resting in the background, as your dream can act as a motivating force.

Unicorn

1 A unicorn in a dream represents the innocent, childlike aspect of yourself, and a sense of wonder. You may be longing to return to that state of innocence after a disappointment, or are feeling jaded and in need of inspiration. A unicorn is a sign to take heart, and be hopeful that matters will improve.
2 In mythology, only the pure of heart and mind were able to meet a unicorn. Your dream indicates that you are actively seeking inner purity, and are connecting more deeply with the spiritual aspects of yourself.

Unicycle

1 Dreaming about a unicycle can indicate a desire to be different, and to 'stand alone' and apart from the crowd. There is an element of showmanship involved in riding a unicycle, and you may be striving for recognition.
2 Your dream may be reminding you to maintain a state of inner balance, as it takes skill to stay aloft on a unicycle. If you are juggling with several projects or ideas, look for a way to hold to your 'centre of gravity'.

Uniform

1 A uniform in dreams represents authority and conformity. Consider the type of uniform, and whether it is you who is wearing it. If you are happy in uniform, you are willing to conform. Casting off a uniform signifies an urge towards independence.
2 Being comfortably part of a group of people wearing uniform indicates that you are ready to identify yourself with a common goal. The sense of unity that this brings reflects a sense of spiritual as well as emotional maturity.

Urine

1 Dreaming that you are passing urine can simply mean that you need to go to the bathroom, and these dreams can often wake you up. Urine can also symbolise your feelings about emotional control. If you are holding it back, this signifies suppressed emotions. Allowing it to flow symbolises an ability to release your feelings.
2 Urination is the body's way of getting rid of toxins or impurities. Dreams about urine can be a reminder to investigate ways of removing yourself from a toxic, or unpleasant, situation. Or it can be a message to consider how to recapture a sense of 'purity' in an element of your life.

Vacancy

1 Dreaming about a vacancy indicates that you are actively searching for opportunities to extend yourself.

2 Are you feeling that something is missing at the moment, and that there is an internal 'gap' that is asking to be filled? Dreaming about a vacancy can be a reminder that you are not tapping into your full potential. The nature of the vacancy in your dream can give clues as to which area of your psyche this involves.

Vacation

1 If you dream about a vacation, you may be feeling under pressure, and need a rest or a break. This dream is usually a reminder to slow down a little, and allow yourself time to focus on pleasure and relaxation.

2 Dreaming of a vacation can be a subconscious message to step away from your usual manner of viewing your life, or a situation, and to approach this from a different, more relaxed perspective. Perhaps your approach has been a little rigid, or you are in need of some spiritual or mental refreshment.

Vagina

1 Dreams of a vagina are less common than sexual dreams, or those involving an opening or tunnel. Vagina dreams are a reminder to be more receptive, as this embodies the traditional female qualities of openness and receptiveness.

2 Whatever your sex, dreaming of a vagina can be a message to consider and embrace your feminine qualities of intuition, gentleness and desire for intimacy. If you have been through a difficult time, this dream may be reflecting a subconscious desire to return to a time of innocence and womblike protection and nurturing.

Vagrant

1 A dream of a vagrant can be an anxiety dream. You may be afraid of losing something that has been hard won, such as a job or relationship, and of the physical or emotional poverty that this would entail.

2 If you dream of a vagrant, you could be feeling out of place, lost, or shunned by someone who is important to you. Giving aid to a vagrant symbolises that you are beginning to nurture elements of yourself that have been neglected or ignored.

Vale

1 Dreaming about a vale, or valley, carries a similar interpretation to that of going down a hill or mountain. If you are travelling down into a vale, this can indicate feelings of depression, or concerns that a situation is 'going downhill', and is worsening. If you are ascending out of the vale, you have sufficient resources to leave behind a difficult time and move on.

2 Dreaming that you are in a sheltered valley can mean that you feel a need to step aside from everyday life, and to retreat to nurture aspects of yourself. Leaving a valley symbolises a return to everyday life after a difficult period. If the vale is dark, this can symbolise subconscious fears about dying.

Valuables

1 Dreaming of valuables signifies an awareness that there are gifts in life that are available to you, if you are willing to reach out and grasp them.

2 Valuables in a dream are related to feelings of self-worth and self-respect. If you find valuables in your dream, this indicates a recovery of these qualities. Losing valuables indicates a loss of confidence, or fear of losing someone or something that is important to you.

Vamp

1 A vamp in a dream carries a predatory element, as a vamp is a woman who is ruled by her sexual nature, and uses this in order to have power or control over others. If you are the vamp, this is a signal to be aware of this aspect of your nature. If someone else is a vamp, you should be careful about trusting the motives of the person whom this represents to you.

2 Dreaming of a vamp can signify that you are struggling to maintain control of your baser desires, or that you have been suppressing these so strongly that your subconscious mind is reminding you of this influence within you.

Vampire

1 Dreaming about a vampire indicates that life-energy is being drained from a situation, and warns you to guard against those who wish to take more from you than you are willing to give. If you are a vampire in your dream, you are taking too much from others. Battling a vampire indicates that you will win out over someone who does not have your best intentions at heart.

2 Is an element of your personality overwhelming other aspects in order to make you feel in control of your life? The vampire can be related to your Shadow, and reflects your deepest fears, or that which is abhorrent to you.

★★

Vase

1 A beautiful vase, or a vase that holds flowers or foliage, signifies a time when you can focus on beauty and creativity. The flowers in the vase can symbolise the elements within yourself that are coming into play. A cracked vase, or one that contains dead or dying flowers, is a message to nurture the relationships in your life.
2 A vase, like any other receptacle, symbolises the emergence of the feminine aspect, regardless of your gender. The qualities of receptiveness, intuition and nurturing are becoming more prevalent when you dream of a vase.

Vault

1 Because a vault usually contains treasure or valuable items, this dream indicates wealth or abundance. If you cannot open the door to a vault, this means that you feel 'locked out' or deprived of the pleasures of life.
2 A vault also symbolises the vast store of knowledge that you hold within you. Dreaming that you are entering a vault signifies that you are now in a position to deepen your understanding of your life, and of your life-purpose.

Vegetable

1 Dreaming about vegetables reflects your feelings about whether your everyday needs are being met. As vegetables are staples in life, you may be concerned that something is currently missing, and are looking for ways in which to be more 'rooted' or secure.
2 The types of vegetables in your dream are significant. Root vegetables such as potatoes or carrots signify a need to become more grounded and earthy in your approach. Plants such as tomatoes remind you to be more aware of love in your life. Exotic vegetables reflect an urge for change or adventure.

Veil

1 Veils in dreams can indicate that something is being kept hidden, or secret. If you are wearing a veil, you are reluctant to disclose too much of yourself to others. Someone else wearing a veil indicates that something is being kept from you.
2 A veil signifies mystery, and can be interpreted as the hidden aspects of yourself. It can also be connected with elements of the occult, and can signify that you are searching for deeper meaning to your life.

Veins

1 Veins symbolise the flow of life-giving energy. Consider your feelings in the dream and any other motifs, as this can indicate which area you need to channel this energy in.
2 Veins in dreams can also represent your deep feelings about your life-force and your pathway in life. Depending upon the context of the dream, veins can mean that you are seeking to tap into your 'vein' of inspiration or inner knowledge, in order to access a greater sense of purpose.

★★★★★★★★★★★★★★★★★★★★★★★★★★★★★★★★★★★★★★

Velvet

1 As a cloth that was once worn only by the very wealthy, velvet signifies abundance, and a focus on gathering prosperity and accomplishment.

2 The soft, sensual feel of velvet can be a subconscious reminder to allow yourself to feel more deeply, and to rely on what your senses are telling you. The colour of the velvet indicates an area or emotion that needs to be expressed.

Vendetta

1 A vendetta is a war between factions. Dreaming of this indicates that there are tensions with others that need to be resolved before damage is done.

2 A vendetta can signify that elements of yourself are pitched against each other. You may be engaged in a battle between your heart and your head. Consider which is winning in your dream, as this is a message to seek inner balance and harmony.

Ventriloquist

1 Are you afraid to speak up for yourself? Dreaming of a ventriloquist can mean that you are relying on someone else to be your 'voice', and express your wishes and needs.

2 An element of your psyche may be used as a conduit for hidden feelings. For instance, you may be expressing anger, when in actuality you are afraid, or deeply hurt. This dream could be a message to allow your inner voice to speak truthfully.

Victim

1 Dreaming that you are a victim indicates feelings of a loss of empowerment or control. If you are rescued by someone in the dream, this indicates a desire to hand over your power to another person, and to give in to feelings of helplessness.

2 A victim dream is a subconscious message that only you can take full responsibility for your life, and that you need to take steps to be more proactive.

Village

1 As a village is a small, close-meshed community, dreaming of this signifies that you feel a need to 'belong', and to find your place in the world. Because there can be few secrets in a village, this can indicate that you wish to be more open, and to be able to trust those around you.

2 You can view the various archetypes within your psyche as being members of a village, of the close-knit community of your mind. The events in the dream can provide clues as to which archetypal elements are currently ruling your life.

★★★★★★★★★★★★★★★★★★★★★★★★★★★★★★★★★★★★★★

Violence
1 Fear, frustration and anxiety can provoke dreams of violence. Consider whether you are the perpetrator or the victim of violence in your dream. If you are on the receiving end, you may be feeling that you are being dealt with unjustly in waking life. Provoking violence in a dream can be a subconscious outlet for anger.
2 Violent dreams are often a result of powerful inner conflict. This dream is a message to consider which elements of yourself are in conflict, and to discover why, in order to attain a state of inner harmony.

Violet
1 A violet is a small flower that, although beautiful, is easily passed by. You may be feeling that you are a 'shrinking violet', and are afraid or reluctant to reveal your true nature. This dream is prompting you to overcome shyness and self-consciousness.
2 You may be forgetting to acknowledge what it is that others find appealing about you. If you dream of violets, this indicates that your unwillingness to accept compliments could be viewed as arrogance. Your dream is reminding you to 'blow your own trumpet'.

Violin
1 If a violin is playing in your dream, this can be a message that romance is in the air.
2 The poignancy of violin music can indicate feelings of sadness that you are reluctant to let go of. The dream is telling you to focus on what is good and beautiful in yourself, and in your life. Like a violin, you have the ability to touch the heart and emotions of others.

Virgin
1 Dreaming of a virgin, whether this is yourself, or someone else, indicates that you are moving onto new and 'untouched' ground in your life. Your dream is telling you that it is time to start afresh, and to look for possibilities and potential.
2 Virginity symbolises a state of purity and innocence that is unaware of and untouched by selfish or coarse considerations. Your dream is a message to focus on maintaining a state of purity of thought; to be true to yourself as well as others.

Visitor
1 A visitor in a dream means that something new is entering your life. Your reaction to the visitor illustrates your response to this change, and will help to ascertain whether you are willing to embrace it, or wish to 'close the door' on it.
2 Dreaming of a visitor signifies that new information is available, which will allow you to open up mentally or spiritually, and will be an important aspect of your growth process. Your Essential Self may take the form of a visitor, if there is information in the dream that contributes to your self-understanding.

★★★★★★★★★★★★★★★★★★★★★★★★★★★★★★★★★★★★★★

Volcano

1 A volcano in a dream indicates that matters have gone out of control, and have taken on a momentum of their own. A volcano is a powerful warning sign, especially if it is erupting.

2 Dreaming of a volcano indicates that you have been repressing or stifling intense emotions. The dream is a message to look for ways in which to release these safely in waking life.

Vomit

1 Vomiting is the body's way of ridding itself of that which is harmful. Dreaming of vomiting indicates that you need to expel someone or something from your life.

2 If you have felt overwhelmed by anxieties or problems, vomiting in a dream is a way of dramatically casting these off. This dream can mean that you have been holding on to destructive feelings such as rage or hatred, and your subconscious mind is ridding itself of them.

Vulture

1 As a scavenger that feeds on the pickings of others, a vulture in dreams is a warning that someone may be helping themselves to what you have gained, and is willing to deprive you of the rewards of your work. If you see yourself as a vulture, you need to be more thoughtful about how you deal with those around you.

2 Dreaming of a vulture can be viewed as a Predator dream, in which your fears of loss are reflected through the Shadow aspect. Consider whether you are taking too much from one aspect of your personality, in order to 'feed' another aspect, and seek ways of redressing the balance.

★★★★★★★★★★★★★★★★★★★★★★★★★★★★★★★★★★★★★★

WADING

1 Dreaming that you are wading indicates that you are now willing to acknowledge your emotions and follow through on your feelings. Wading through clear water means that you are feeling good about your emotional life. Muddy water indicates a reluctance to explore your feelings.

2 Wading in dreams symbolises a conscious desire to immerse yourself in the experience of life. If the act of wading seems like an effort in your dream, you are pushing yourself to set new experiences in motion. Wading easily signifies that you are ready to fully immerse yourself in life.

WAITING

1 Dreaming that you are waiting indicates your feelings about a delay in a situation. If you are waiting patiently, you are prepared to 'sit' the situation out. Impatience or irritation in the dream signifies a desire to forge ahead, and possible irritation with something or someone that is holding you back in waking life.

2 Your subconscious mind may be telling you to hold back on a decision, to 'wait and see' rather than rush in.

WALKING

1 Walking symbolises the way in which you are moving towards a goal. If you are relaxed and are enjoying the scenery, this means that you are willing to take in all aspects of a situation. If you need support, in the form of a staff or walking stick, this indicates a need to ask for help in order to make progress.

2 Walking in a dream can signify your journey through life. Consider how you are walking, and your feelings in the dream. If you are striding ahead, this means that you are 'taking steps' determinedly towards your goal. Dragging your feet signifies a reluctance to take the 'next step' in a situation.

WALL

1 A wall in a dream indicates that you are facing a barrier or obstacle, and a wall keeps you in (and safe) or shuts you out and excludes you. Consider the nature of the wall, and whether it is made of it brick or stone. A sea defence indicates that you are building a wall against your emotions.

2 Dreaming of a wall indicates that you are putting up a mental barrier. You may be faced with ideas that you dislike. A wall signifies a need to be more open and accepting in your attitudes.

Wallet

1 Dreaming about a wallet indicates that you are focused on your financial resources. If you find a wallet, this signifies an improvement in your situation. Losing your wallet signifies that you are concerned about a financial problem.
2 Like a 'purse', a wallet in a dream is also symbolic of your feelings about your identity, as it contains items such as credit cards or identity passes that make a statement about who you are and how you define yourself.

War

1 If you have been involved in the military, a war dream can be your mind's way of reliving an experience, and integrating your feelings around this. War dreams can occur when there is intense conflict with a person or institution, and the outcome in the dream is significant, as this can be a key as to how to move forward.
2 The war in your dream could be between elements within your psyche, as in a 'battle' dream. You may be in a situation of inner conflict. Consider the factions in the dream war, and how you can relate this to any internal upheaval.

Warehouse

1 A warehouse is a storage space for that which is no longer needed or which is being set aside for future use. Dreaming of this can indicate that you are in the process of trawling through past memories, and sifting what is practically useable for the future.
2 A warehouse in a dream can be a repository for spiritual insights as well as intellectual information. It can symbolise the vast storehouse of the mind, in which nothing is ever truly forgotten.

Washing

1 If you are washing clothes in your dream, this indicates a need to freshen up your outward appearance, and the persona that you present to the world. Washing dishes signifies that it is important to pay attention to your diet and nutrition.
2 If you are washing yourself in a dream, this means that you are 'washing away' negative attitudes, or unhelpful beliefs or philosophies, and are engaging in a process of 'cleaning up your act'. Washing in dreams signifies a deliberate self-purification.

Watch

1 As with 'clock' dreams, a watch signifies an awareness of the passage of time. As a watch is usually worn on the wrist, and is instantly accessible, this indicates that you are focusing on keeping to a specific time-frame. You may be working towards a deadline, or waiting for an anticipated event to occur.
2 You may be 'watchful' and alert for information or an event if you dream of a watch. Or your dream could be a signal to 'watch out' for problems, and is a warning message. Your feelings within the dream will give you clues as to its interpretation.

★★★★★★★★★★★★★★★★★★★★★★★★★★★★★★★★★★★★★★

Water

1 Water in dreams always represents an element of your emotions. The nature of the water is significant. Consider whether this is in the form of a glass of water, symbolising a taking-in of life-force, or whether this is a pool, river, lake, waterfall or flood. Your feelings within the dream are important to the interpretation.
2 The condition of the water will enable you to decipher your attitude towards your emotional involvement. Murky water indicates confusion or anxiety. Clear water symbolises emotional clarity and positivity. Dammed water can indicate that you have been 'bottling things up' and need to break down an emotional blockage.

Waterfall

1 A waterfall in a dream signifies an outpouring and overflowing of emotions that is viewed as positive and even blissful or sensual. You may have been feeling overwhelmed, but have given yourself over to the intensity of an emotional experience and can enjoy its beauty and force.
2 If you have been holding back your emotions, a dream of a waterfall is a safe way in which your subconscious mind allows these to spill out and be more comfortably dealt with. A waterfall in dreams can also signify spiritual purification and cleansing.

Weapon

1 A weapon in dreams signifies a desire to hurt someone or something. If you are wielding the weapon, you should examine your motives in wishing to cause harm. If a weapon is being used on you, this indicates that you feel 'under attack' from someone.
2 The type of weapon is significant. A sharp object such as a knife or sword represents the cutting edge of the intellect. A gun symbolises a desire to 'blast away' opposition. An arrow represents the urge to 'pierce through' to the heart of a matter.

Web

1 There are similarities between dreams of a web, and 'spider' dreams. You may be feeling enmeshed within a situation or relationship that appears to be difficult to escape from.
2 A web in dreams can also be the intermeshing of thoughts and insights, and a realisation of the interconnectedness of all of life.

Wedding

1 Dreaming of a wedding may mean that you are focusing on a literal wedding that is about to take place. Or it can indicate a desire for commitment in a relationship.
2 A dream wedding can be symbolic of the 'marriage' of different aspects of yourself. It can symbolise the union of the Anima and Animus, the male and female aspects, or can be a union of ideas that are now merging to create a cohesive structure.

★★★

Weeds

1 Weeds in dreams indicate that you feel 'choked up' with extraneous junk in your life. If you are engaged in weeding, this reveals an inclination to rid yourself of what is no longer useful to you. A garden full of weeds can mean that you are neglecting to focus on your creative aspect.

2 Weeds can also symbolise a 'weeding out' process that is taking place within you. You may be deliberately casting aside old ideas or habits, and are undergoing an internal 'spring clean'.

Well

1 A well symbolises the deepest resources of your inner being and emotions. If the well is easy to access, this indicates that you are able to tap into the 'wellspring' of your life, and make full use of your resources and potential. If you fall into a well, this indicates that you fear a loss of control, or are 'out of your depth' emotionally. A dried-up well signifies that you feel that you have run out of inspiration and resources.

2 A well in dreams can also be a metaphor for emotional, physical and spiritual 'wellness'. Your dream could be reminding you to take a holistic approach to your health and care for all aspects of yourself.

Whale

1 As the largest cetacean, a whale indicates that you are dealing with 'big' emotional issues that are in need of careful communication in order to be resolved. It can mean that you are having a 'whale' of a time, and setting yourself up for some fun.

2 Because whales are gentle mammals which live in the sea, dreaming of whales can indicate a spiritual rebirth or resurrection process, especially if the whales are 'singing'.

Whirlpool

1 If you dream of a whirlpool, your emotions are in a state of upheaval, and you are being 'sucked into' a situation that is not healthy for you.

2 A whirlpool can be a symbol of tremendous emotional power; too much to control. You may be attempting to control something that is a 'natural force', and is spurred on by its own momentum. This can be a positive dream if your feelings are those of excitement, or negative if you feel panicky and afraid.

White

1 White is the colour associated with purity. If your dream is predominantly in white, this indicates a desire to build on what is pure and wholesome in your life.

2 The colour white is composed of a blend of every colour in the spectrum. Dreaming of white signifies a growing connection with the spiritual aspect of your nature, and the desire for a state of unity and wholeness.

A B C D E F G H I J K L M N O P Q R S T U V W X Y Z

Wife

1 For a married man, dreams of a wife can reflect his wishes, desires or fears around close relationships. For a woman, the dream can reflect her feelings about her role in a relationship, or with close friends.

2 A 'wife' dream can indicate that your caring, nurturing aspect is coming to the surface, or that you are ready to enter into a partnership – either romantic or business – in which you carry a supportive role.

Will

1 If you are making or reading a will in a dream, this signifies that you wish to plan out important matters in your life, and leave nothing to chance. Because a will is a legal, binding document, your dream can signify a lasting commitment to an issue that is important to you.

2 Dreaming about a will can be message that you need to muster up the 'will' to act in a situation that you may have been procrastinating over.

Willow tree

1 A tree in a dream signifies your approach to life, and as in 'tree' dreams, the part of the tree is significant. Because of the willow's affinity to water, and the use of its bark to create the drug aspirin, this tree symbolises that a healing process is taking place.

2 Your dream may be telling you to be more emotionally flexible, as a willow is able to bend with the wind.

Wind

1 The condition of the wind, and your feelings about it, are significant. If you are struggling against a strong wind, you are battling with a situation that is taking a great deal of energy. A fair wind that blows you along indicates a smooth passage towards your goal.

2 The wind in dreams symbolises your thought processes, and the manner in which the wind blows represents how you are acting on those thoughts in your waking life. Wind dreams often occur during times of transition and change, when you need to adjust your way of thinking.

Window

1 Dreaming of a window is symbolic of your perspective on life and the world around you. If the window is open, this indicates that you wish to connect more with what is 'outside' or beyond yourself. A closed window signifies a barrier between yourself and the outside world. If you are outside looking in, you are feeling left out or excluded.

2 A dream of a window can be a window into your inner thoughts and motivations, and into the depths of your being and your soul. This dream can indicate that you are becoming more introspective and are engaged in thinking about deep issues.

Wine

1 Dreaming about wine can signify fertility and fruitfulness, and happiness. Because wine is often shared at a gathering of people, this dream signals a celebration. As with 'alcohol' and 'drinking' dreams, a dream about wine can be message to loosen up a little, to relax and allow yourself to enjoy life.
2 Wine can symbolise spiritual gifts, and a realisation of the innate abundance of the universe.

Wings

1 If you dream of wings, you may be about to 'take off', and realise your dreams. Wings symbolise flight and freedom. A broken wing signifies sorrow, or the gradual slowing down of a situation or relationship which is coming to an end. There are similarities between wings dreams and flight dreams.
2 Wings in dreams can symbolise spiritual energy, as in the soul that takes flight, and spiritual protection, because of the common perception of angels with wings.

Winter

1 Dreaming of winter indicates a dormant period, where plans are 'frozen' for the time being. Consider whether you should allow some time to 'hibernate' and reflect on where you headed. Winter dreams can also signify emotional coldness, and a frosty withdrawal.
2 As the seasons in dreams are associated with the seasons in a life-cycle, winter indicates the wisdom and maturity of old age, and possibly death.

Witch

1 Your feelings about the witch in your dream are important to your interpretation. A 'wicked witch' can indicate fears and anxieties about a situation or person who is causing you concern. A 'good witch' symbolises self-empowerment, help and healing.
2 A witch in dreams can symbolise the fully empowered feminine aspect, and a feeling of control over the circumstances of your life. You may be feeling that a situation is 'magical', or that you have a 'fairy godmother'.

Wolf

1 A wolf in Native lore symbolises wisdom, knowledge, and the ability to draw the 'pack' or 'clan' together, and keep it cohesive. The family is very important to a wolf, and it will sacrifice itself for its young, so your dream signifies a powerful connection with others. A solitary wolf indicates that you feel a need to forge ahead alone, though this may be a sad time for you.
2 As an aspect of the wild Self, dreams of a wolf can be a message to tap into your own instinctive nature.

★★★★★★★★★★★★★★★★★★★★★★★★★★★★★★★★★★★★★★

Womb

1 If you dream of a womb, you are inwardly yearning to be nurtured, nourished and looked after in a protective space. There is a need to connect with the innocent, pure aspect of yourself at this time, as womb dreams often occur when you are sad or disillusioned, antd wish to retreat from the cares of the world.

2 The womb signifies the conception of an idea, and the care and nurturing that is important for its gestation and birth into the light of day. A womb in dreams is the ultimate creative space.

Writing

1 Consider what material the writing is on in your dream. A written scroll or parchment indicates ancient knowledge or understanding coming to the fore. The 'writing on the wall' can be a message to let go of a situation that carries little chance of success.

2 Writing in dreams is a direct communication from the subconscious and unconscious mind. This can be a powerful message that can show you the best direction to take at this time.

X-RAY

1 Dreaming about an x-ray can indicate concerns about your health. It can also symbolise introspection, and a desire to 'see through' a situation, and access what is hidden beneath surface matters.

2 Consider the part of the body that is being x-rayed. Your chest indicates a need to examine your feelings, and what inspires you. A limb indicates a desire to understand what can move you forward. An x-ray of your head signifies a need to think clearly.

YELLOW

1 Yellow is the colour associated with sunshine, positive feelings, and warmth. Your dream is reminding you to focus on these, and may be a message that success and happiness are coming to you.

2 Yellow is also the colour that symbolises the intellect. You may be stretching yourself intellectually, and are enjoying the mental growth process that this brings.

YEW

1 Yew trees are planted in graveyards, and carry an association with death and rebirth. If you dream of a yew tree, you may be facing deeply hidden fears or anxieties about death.

2 The feelings of sadness that are often connected with yew trees can indicate that you are 'wallowing' in negative emotions, and need to turn your attention outwards.

YOGI

1 Dreaming of a yogi indicates a desire to seek advice from someone who has a spiritual as well as a wise outlook.

2 A yogi in dreams can be a manifestation of the wise aspect of yourself, which combines authority and good sense with a spiritual perspective. Your interaction with the yogi in your dream indicates how you relate to this aspect of yourself.

YOLK

1 The yolk of an egg contains the new life that is nourished by the albumin surrounding it. Your dream may be reminding you to focus on inner rather than external nurturing and nourishment.

2 Dreaming of a yolk can also signify that you feel contained or trapped, as in the yolk that binds animals together. Consider whether you are feeling held back by an attitude within yourself, or are bound so closely to another person that there is no room for freedom of 'movement'.

★★★★★★★★★★★★★★★★★★★★★★★★★★★★★★★★★★★★★★

Youth

1 The behaviour of the youth in your dream is significant. A friendly youth indicates that you are ready to embark a new phase of life, and view this as an adventure. A hostile youth can represent the rebellious aspect of your nature coming to the fore.
2 Dreaming of a youth, in the context of age being related to life cycles, indicates that you wish to have more fun, and to have a more carefree attitude towards life. Dreams of youth can signify a desire to escape from responsibility.

Zebra

1 A zebra in a dream has a similar interpretation to that of a horse. Its swiftness of movement indicates a desire to move forward, and to add impetus to the energy that you are gathering for your undertakings.
2 Whereas a horse can be tamed and ridden for pleasure, or used to pull heavy loads, a zebra is a wild creature. Your dream may be warning you that others will not cooperate as much as you wish them to.

Zip

1 Consider whether the zip is open or closed. A zip can signify communication with others. If the zip is open, the lines of communication are clear. If it is closed, a shutting-down process is occurring. A stuck or jammed zip means that you are in an awkward or embarrassing situation.
2 A zip can also symbolise a desire for unity, and a need to pull diverse elements or ideas together in order to create a cohesive whole. Undoing a zip can indicate a need to leave behind outgrown beliefs or ideas.

Zoo

1 If you dream of a zoo, you may be feeling caged or imprisoned in a situation. Your feelings in the dream are vital to its interpretation, as a zoo can also be a place of recreation and relaxation.
2 Dreaming about a zoo can be a message from your subconscious mind that reminds you to focus on understanding your natural instincts. You may have been ignoring your instinctive, intuitive self, in favour of logic and reasoning. Another message in this dream is a reminder to observe those around you, in order to learn from them.

Dream Diary

Dream 1

Date ....

What was the dream story?

....

....

....

....

Were you a participant or an observer in the dream?

....

What were your actions or reactions to events?

....

....

....

What were the main characters and images?

....

....

....

Were any of the dream characters familiar to you?

....

....

Did anything in the dream strike you as particularly significant?

....

....

Where or when was the dream set?

....

....

How did the dream make you feel?

....

....

Your interpretation

....

....

....

....

Dream 2

Date ....

What was the dream story?

....

....

....

....

Were you a participant or an observer in the dream?

....

What were your actions or reactions to events?

....

....

....

What were the main characters and images?

....

....

....

Were any of the dream characters familiar to you?

....

....

Did anything in the dream strike you as particularly significant?

....

....

Where or when was the dream set?

....

....

How did the dream make you feel?

....

....

Your interpretation

....

....

....

....

Dream 3 Date ....

What was the dream story?

....

....

....

....

Were you a participant or an observer in the dream?

....

What were your actions or reactions to events?

....

....

....

What were the main characters and images?

....

....

....

Were any of the dream characters familiar to you?

....

....

Did anything in the dream strike you as particularly significant?

....

....

Where or when was the dream set?

....

....

How did the dream make you feel?

....

....

Your interpretation

....

....

....

....

Dream 4 Date ....

What was the dream story?

....

....

....

....

Were you a participant or an observer in the dream?

....

What were your actions or reactions to events?

....

....

....

What were the main characters and images?

....

....

....

Were any of the dream characters familiar to you?

....

....

Did anything in the dream strike you as particularly significant?

....

....

Where or when was the dream set?

....

....

How did the dream make you feel?

....

....

Your interpretation

....

....

....

....

Dream 5

Date ....

What was the dream story?

....

....

....

....

Were you a participant or an observer in the dream?

....

What were your actions or reactions to events?

....

....

....

What were the main characters and images?

....

....

....

Were any of the dream characters familiar to you?

....

....

Did anything in the dream strike you as particularly significant?

....

....

Where or when was the dream set?

....

....

How did the dream make you feel?

....

....

Your interpretation

....

....

....

....

Dream 6

Date ....

What was the dream story?

....

....

....

....

Were you a participant or an observer in the dream?

....

What were your actions or reactions to events?

....

....

....

What were the main characters and images?

....

....

....

Were any of the dream characters familiar to you?

....

....

Did anything in the dream strike you as particularly significant?

....

....

Where or when was the dream set?

....

....

How did the dream make you feel?

....

....

Your interpretation

....

....

....

....

Dream 7 Date ....

What was the dream story?

....

....

....

....

Were you a participant or an observer in the dream?

....

What were your actions or reactions to events?

....

....

....

What were the main characters and images?

....

....

....

Were any of the dream characters familiar to you?

....

....

Did anything in the dream strike you as particularly significant?

....

....

Where or when was the dream set?

....

....

How did the dream make you feel?

....

....

Your interpretation

....

....

....

....

Dream 8 Date ....

What was the dream story?

....

....

....

....

Were you a participant or an observer in the dream?

....

What were your actions or reactions to events?

....

....

....

What were the main characters and images?

....

....

....

Were any of the dream characters familiar to you?

....

....

Did anything in the dream strike you as particularly significant?

....

....

Where or when was the dream set?

....

....

How did the dream make you feel?

....

....

Your interpretation

....

....

....

....

Dream 9 Date ....

What was the dream story?

Were you a participant or an observer in the dream?

What were your actions or reactions to events?

What were the main characters and images?

Were any of the dream characters familiar to you?

Did anything in the dream strike you as particularly significant?

Where or when was the dream set?

How did the dream make you feel?

Your interpretation

Dream 10 Date ....

What was the dream story?

Were you a participant or an observer in the dream?

What were your actions or reactions to events?

What were the main characters and images?

Were any of the dream characters familiar to you?

Did anything in the dream strike you as particularly significant?

Where or when was the dream set?

How did the dream make you feel?

Your interpretation

Dream 11 Date ....

What was the dream story?

Were you a participant or an observer in the dream?

What were your actions or reactions to events?

What were the main characters and images?

Were any of the dream characters familiar to you?

Did anything in the dream strike you as particularly significant?

Where or when was the dream set?

How did the dream make you feel?

Your interpretation

Dream 12 Date ....

What was the dream story?

Were you a participant or an observer in the dream?

What were your actions or reactions to events?

What were the main characters and images?

Were any of the dream characters familiar to you?

Did anything in the dream strike you as particularly significant?

Where or when was the dream set?

How did the dream make you feel?

Your interpretation

Dream 13 Date ....

What was the dream story?

....

....

....

....

Were you a participant or an observer in the dream?

....

What were your actions or reactions to events?

....

....

....

What were the main characters and images?

....

....

....

Were any of the dream characters familiar to you?

....

....

Did anything in the dream strike you as particularly significant?

....

....

Where or when was the dream set?

....

....

How did the dream make you feel?

....

....

Your interpretation

....

....

....

....

Dream 14 Date ....

What was the dream story?

....

....

....

....

Were you a participant or an observer in the dream?

....

What were your actions or reactions to events?

....

....

....

What were the main characters and images?

....

....

....

Were any of the dream characters familiar to you?

....

....

Did anything in the dream strike you as particularly significant?

....

....

Where or when was the dream set?

....

....

How did the dream make you feel?

....

....

Your interpretation

....

....

....

....

Dream 15 Date ....

What was the dream story?

....

....

....

....

Were you a participant or an observer in the dream?

....

What were your actions or reactions to events?

....

....

....

What were the main characters and images?

....

....

....

Were any of the dream characters familiar to you?

....

....

Did anything in the dream strike you as particularly significant?

....

....

Where or when was the dream set?

....

....

How did the dream make you feel?

....

....

Your interpretation

....

....

....

....

Dream 16 Date ....

What was the dream story?

....

....

....

....

Were you a participant or an observer in the dream?

....

What were your actions or reactions to events?

....

....

....

What were the main characters and images?

....

....

....

Were any of the dream characters familiar to you?

....

....

Did anything in the dream strike you as particularly significant?

....

....

Where or when was the dream set?

....

....

How did the dream make you feel?

....

....

Your interpretation

....

....

....

....

Dream 17 Date ....

What was the dream story?

....

Were you a participant or an observer in the dream?

....

What were your actions or reactions to events?

....

What were the main characters and images?

....

Were any of the dream characters familiar to you?

....

Did anything in the dream strike you as particularly significant?

....

Where or when was the dream set?

....

How did the dream make you feel?

....

Your interpretation

....

Dream 18 Date ....

What was the dream story?

....

Were you a participant or an observer in the dream?

....

What were your actions or reactions to events?

....

What were the main characters and images?

....

Were any of the dream characters familiar to you?

....

Did anything in the dream strike you as particularly significant?

....

Where or when was the dream set?

....

How did the dream make you feel?

....

Your interpretation

....

Dream 19 Date ....

What was the dream story?

....

Were you a participant or an observer in the dream?

....

What were your actions or reactions to events?

....

What were the main characters and images?

....

Were any of the dream characters familiar to you?

....

Did anything in the dream strike you as particularly significant?

....

Where or when was the dream set?

....

How did the dream make you feel?

....

Your interpretation

....

Dream 20 Date ....

What was the dream story?

....

Were you a participant or an observer in the dream?

....

What were your actions or reactions to events?

....

What were the main characters and images?

....

Were any of the dream characters familiar to you?

....

Did anything in the dream strike you as particularly significant?

....

Where or when was the dream set?

....

How did the dream make you feel?

....

Your interpretation

....

Dream 21 Date ....

What was the dream story?

...

Were you a participant or an observer in the dream?

...

What were your actions or reactions to events?

...

What were the main characters and images?

...

Were any of the dream characters familiar to you?

...

Did anything in the dream strike you as particularly significant?

...

Where or when was the dream set?

...

How did the dream make you feel?

...

Your interpretation

...

Dream 22 Date ....

What was the dream story?

...

Were you a participant or an observer in the dream?

...

What were your actions or reactions to events?

...

What were the main characters and images?

...

Were any of the dream characters familiar to you?

...

Did anything in the dream strike you as particularly significant?

...

Where or when was the dream set?

...

How did the dream make you feel?

...

Your interpretation

...

Dream 23 Date ....

What was the dream story?

Were you a participant or an observer in the dream?

What were your actions or reactions to events?

What were the main characters and images?

Were any of the dream characters familiar to you?

Did anything in the dream strike you as particularly significant?

Where or when was the dream set?

How did the dream make you feel?

Your interpretation

Dream 24 Date ....

What was the dream story?

Were you a participant or an observer in the dream?

What were your actions or reactions to events?

What were the main characters and images?

Were any of the dream characters familiar to you?

Did anything in the dream strike you as particularly significant?

Where or when was the dream set?

How did the dream make you feel?

Your interpretation

Dream 25 Date ....

What was the dream story?

....

....

....

....

Were you a participant or an observer in the dream?

....

What were your actions or reactions to events?

....

....

....

What were the main characters and images?

....

....

....

Were any of the dream characters familiar to you?

....

....

Did anything in the dream strike you as particularly significant?

....

....

Where or when was the dream set?

....

....

How did the dream make you feel?

....

....

Your interpretation

....

....

....

....

Dream 26 Date ....

What was the dream story?

....

....

....

....

Were you a participant or an observer in the dream?

....

What were your actions or reactions to events?

....

....

....

What were the main characters and images?

....

....

....

Were any of the dream characters familiar to you?

....

....

Did anything in the dream strike you as particularly significant?

....

....

Where or when was the dream set?

....

....

How did the dream make you feel?

....

....

Your interpretation

....

....

....

....

Dream 27 Date ....

What was the dream story?

....

....

....

....

Were you a participant or an observer in the dream?

....

What were your actions or reactions to events?

....

....

....

What were the main characters and images?

....

....

....

Were any of the dream characters familiar to you?

....

....

Did anything in the dream strike you as particularly significant?

....

....

Where or when was the dream set?

....

....

How did the dream make you feel?

....

....

Your interpretation

....

....

....

....

Dream 28 Date ....

What was the dream story?

....

....

....

....

Were you a participant or an observer in the dream?

....

What were your actions or reactions to events?

....

....

....

What were the main characters and images?

....

....

....

Were any of the dream characters familiar to you?

....

....

Did anything in the dream strike you as particularly significant?

....

....

Where or when was the dream set?

....

....

How did the dream make you feel?

....

....

Your interpretation

....

....

....

....

Dream 29 Date ....

What was the dream story?

Were you a participant or an observer in the dream?

What were your actions or reactions to events?

What were the main characters and images?

Were any of the dream characters familiar to you?

Did anything in the dream strike you as particularly significant?

Where or when was the dream set?

How did the dream make you feel?

Your interpretation

Dream 30 Date ....

What was the dream story?

Were you a participant or an observer in the dream?

What were your actions or reactions to events?

What were the main characters and images?

Were any of the dream characters familiar to you?

Did anything in the dream strike you as particularly significant?

Where or when was the dream set?

How did the dream make you feel?

Your interpretation

Dream 31 Date ....

What was the dream story?

....

....

....

....

Were you a participant or an observer in the dream?

....

What were your actions or reactions to events?

....

....

....

What were the main characters and images?

....

....

....

Were any of the dream characters familiar to you?

....

....

Did anything in the dream strike you as particularly significant?

....

....

Where or when was the dream set?

....

....

How did the dream make you feel?

....

....

Your interpretation

....

....

....

....

Dream 32 Date ....

What was the dream story?

....

....

....

....

Were you a participant or an observer in the dream?

....

What were your actions or reactions to events?

....

....

....

What were the main characters and images?

....

....

....

Were any of the dream characters familiar to you?

....

....

Did anything in the dream strike you as particularly significant?

....

....

Where or when was the dream set?

....

....

How did the dream make you feel?

....

....

Your interpretation

....

....

....

....

Dream 33 Date ....

What was the dream story?

....

....

....

....

Were you a participant or an observer in the dream?

....

What were your actions or reactions to events?

....

....

....

What were the main characters and images?

....

....

....

Were any of the dream characters familiar to you?

....

....

Did anything in the dream strike you as particularly significant?

....

....

Where or when was the dream set?

....

....

How did the dream make you feel?

....

....

Your interpretation

....

....

....

....

Dream 34 Date ....

What was the dream story?

....

....

....

....

Were you a participant or an observer in the dream?

....

What were your actions or reactions to events?

....

....

....

What were the main characters and images?

....

....

....

Were any of the dream characters familiar to you?

....

....

Did anything in the dream strike you as particularly significant?

....

....

Where or when was the dream set?

....

....

How did the dream make you feel?

....

....

Your interpretation

....

....

....

....

Dream 35 Date ....

What was the dream story?

....

....

....

....

Were you a participant or an observer in the dream?

....

What were your actions or reactions to events?

....

....

....

What were the main characters and images?

....

....

....

Were any of the dream characters familiar to you?

....

....

Did anything in the dream strike you as particularly significant?

....

....

Where or when was the dream set?

....

....

How did the dream make you feel?

....

....

Your interpretation

....

....

....

....

Dream 36 Date ....

What was the dream story?

....

....

....

....

Were you a participant or an observer in the dream?

....

What were your actions or reactions to events?

....

....

....

What were the main characters and images?

....

....

....

Were any of the dream characters familiar to you?

....

....

Did anything in the dream strike you as particularly significant?

....

....

Where or when was the dream set?

....

....

How did the dream make you feel?

....

....

Your interpretation

....

....

....

....

Dream 37 Date ....

What was the dream story?

....

....

....

....

Were you a participant or an observer in the dream?

....

What were your actions or reactions to events?

....

....

....

What were the main characters and images?

....

....

....

Were any of the dream characters familiar to you?

....

....

Did anything in the dream strike you as particularly significant?

....

....

Where or when was the dream set?

....

....

How did the dream make you feel?

....

....

Your interpretation

....

....

....

....

Dream 38 Date ....

What was the dream story?

....

....

....

....

Were you a participant or an observer in the dream?

....

What were your actions or reactions to events?

....

....

....

What were the main characters and images?

....

....

....

Were any of the dream characters familiar to you?

....

....

Did anything in the dream strike you as particularly significant?

....

....

Where or when was the dream set?

....

....

How did the dream make you feel?

....

....

Your interpretation

....

....

....

....

Dream 39 Date ....

What was the dream story?

....

....

....

....

Were you a participant or an observer in the dream?

....

What were your actions or reactions to events?

....

....

....

What were the main characters and images?

....

....

....

Were any of the dream characters familiar to you?

....

....

Did anything in the dream strike you as particularly significant?

....

....

Where or when was the dream set?

....

....

How did the dream make you feel?

....

....

Your interpretation

....

....

....

....

Dream 40 Date ....

What was the dream story?

....

....

....

....

Were you a participant or an observer in the dream?

....

What were your actions or reactions to events?

....

....

....

What were the main characters and images?

....

....

....

Were any of the dream characters familiar to you?

....

....

Did anything in the dream strike you as particularly significant?

....

....

Where or when was the dream set?

....

....

How did the dream make you feel?

....

....

Your interpretation

....

....

....

....

Dream 41 Date ....

What was the dream story?

Were you a participant or an observer in the dream?

What were your actions or reactions to events?

What were the main characters and images?

Were any of the dream characters familiar to you?

Did anything in the dream strike you as particularly significant?

Where or when was the dream set?

How did the dream make you feel?

Your interpretation

Dream 42 Date ....

What was the dream story?

Were you a participant or an observer in the dream?

What were your actions or reactions to events?

What were the main characters and images?

Were any of the dream characters familiar to you?

Did anything in the dream strike you as particularly significant?

Where or when was the dream set?

How did the dream make you feel?

Your interpretation

Dream 43 Date ....

What was the dream story?

...

Were you a participant or an observer in the dream?

What were your actions or reactions to events?

What were the main characters and images?

Were any of the dream characters familiar to you?

Did anything in the dream strike you as particularly significant?

Where or when was the dream set?

How did the dream make you feel?

Your interpretation

Dream 44 Date ....

What was the dream story?

Were you a participant or an observer in the dream?

What were your actions or reactions to events?

What were the main characters and images?

Were any of the dream characters familiar to you?

Did anything in the dream strike you as particularly significant?

Where or when was the dream set?

How did the dream make you feel?

Your interpretation

Dream 45 Date ....

What was the dream story?

....

....

....

....

Were you a participant or an observer in the dream?

....

What were your actions or reactions to events?

....

....

....

What were the main characters and images?

....

....

....

Were any of the dream characters familiar to you?

....

....

Did anything in the dream strike you as particularly significant?

....

....

Where or when was the dream set?

....

....

How did the dream make you feel?

....

....

Your interpretation

....

....

....

....

Dream 46 Date ....

What was the dream story?

....

....

....

....

Were you a participant or an observer in the dream?

....

What were your actions or reactions to events?

....

....

....

What were the main characters and images?

....

....

....

Were any of the dream characters familiar to you?

....

....

Did anything in the dream strike you as particularly significant?

....

....

Where or when was the dream set?

....

....

How did the dream make you feel?

....

....

Your interpretation

....

....

....

....